BE COMMITTED

Be Committed

WARREN W. WIERSBE

Victor®

The Bible Teacher's Teacher

COOK COMMUNICATIONS MINISTRIES
Colorado Springs, Colorado • Paris, Ontario
KINGSWAY COMMUNICATIONS LTD
Eastbourne, England

Victor® is an imprint of
Cook Communications Ministries, Colorado Springs, CO 80918
Cook Communications, Paris, Ontario
Kingsway Communications, Eastbourne, England

BE COMMITTED
© 1993 by SP PUBLICATIONS, INC.
© 2005 by COOK COMMUNICATIONS MINISTRIES

Printed in the United States of America
12 13 14 15 16

Cover Photo: © PhotoDisc Inc.
Cover Design: Joe DeLeon
Copyediting: Jerry Yamamoto and Barbara Williams

Library of Congress Cataloging-in-Publication Data
Wiersbe, Warren W.
        Be committed / by Warren W. Wiersbe.
            p. cm.
        Includes bibliographical references.
        ISBN: 978-1-56476-067-8
        1. Ruth (Biblical character)–Meditations.   2. Esther, Queen of
        Persia–Meditations.   3. Bible. O.T. Ruth–Meditations.   4. Bible. O.T.
        Esther–Meditations.   5. Women in the Bible–Meditations.
        I. Title
        BS580.R8W54   1993
        222'.3506–dc20

                                                                    92-34114
                                                                       CIP

CONTENTS

The Book of Ruth

The Book of Esther

PREFACE

Dr. Ruth A. Tucker and Dr. Walter Liefeld come to this conclusion in their outstanding book *Daughters of the Church:*

> Questions about authority in the church, and particularly about the ministry of women, might be resolved more biblically if attention were given to the fact that "ministry" means "serving." With that definition in mind, a most appropriate response . . . is not for either men or women to grasp at ministerial status or authority, but rather to encourage one another in faithful service to the glory of God (p. 441).

That's what Ruth and Esther do for me. They encourage me to be faithful in my service to the glory of the Lord. At an hour in history when it's easy to compromise and even to quit, these two heroines of the faith tell me to be committed to the Lord and to do the will of God, come what may.

Now that these chapters are finished, I confess that I didn't feel worthy even to write about these two women. But I trust that what I've written has been accurate and fair, and that these chapters will help you in your commitment to the Lord Jesus Christ.

Warren W. Wiersbe

The Book of Ruth

PRELUDE

Ruth and Esther are the only women in the Old Testament who have entire books devoted to them. The Book of Ruth tells the story of a Gentile who married a Jew and became an ancestress of the Messiah (Matt. 1:5). The Book of Esther introduces us to a Jewess who married a Gentile and was used of God to save the Jewish nation from destruction so that the Messiah could be born.

The story of Ruth begins with a famine and ends with the birth of a baby, while the story of Esther begins with a feast and ends with the death of over 75,000 people. God is mentioned twenty-five times in the Book of Ruth, but He is not named even once in all the Book of Esther! Yet in both books, the will of God is fulfilled and the providential hand of God is clearly seen.

Why do we bring these two women together in this study? Because, in spite of their different backgrounds and experiences, *both Ruth and Esther were committed to do the will of God.* Ruth's reply to Naomi (Ruth 1:16-17) is one of the great confessions of faith found in Scripture, and Esther's reply to Mordecai (Es. 4:16) reveals a woman willing to lay down her life to save her people. Ruth and Esther both summon Christians today to be committed to Jesus Christ and to do His will at any cost.

It has well been said that faith is not believing in spite of evidence but obeying in spite of consequence. Ruth and Esther point the way to that kind of dynamic and exciting faith, and we do well to follow their example.

A Suggested Outline of the Book of Ruth

Theme: God providentially guides and blesses all who trust
       Him
Theme verse: Ruth 2:12

I. Sorrow: Ruth Weeping — chap. 1
1. Naomi tries to run from her problems — 1:1-5
2. Naomi tries to cover up her mistakes — 1:6-18
3. Naomi gets bitter against God — 1:19-22

II. Service: Ruth Working — chap. 2
1. A new beginning — faith — 2:1-3
2. A new friend — love — 2:4-16
3. A new attitude — hope — 2:17-23

III. Submission: Ruth Waiting — chap. 3
1. Ruth presents herself to Boaz — 3:1-7
2. Ruth is accepted by Boaz — 3:8-15
3. Ruth waits for Boaz to act — 3:16-18

IV. Satisfaction: Ruth Wedding — chap. 4
1. Boaz redeems Ruth — 4:1-10
2. The people bless Ruth — 4:11-12
3. God gives Boaz and Ruth a son — 4:13-22

You Can't Run Away

(In which a family makes a bad decision
and exchanges one famine for three funerals)

The efforts which we make to escape from our destiny only serve to lead us into it."

The American essayist Ralph Waldo Emerson wrote that in his book *The Conduct of Life,* and it's just as true today as when the book was published back in 1860. Because God gave us freedom of choice, we can ignore the will of God, argue with it, disobey it, even fight against it. But in the end, the will of God shall prevail; because "the counsel of the Lord stands forever" (Ps. 33:11) and "He does according to His will in the army of heaven and among the inhabitants of the earth" (Dan. 4:35, NKJV).

The patriarch Job asked, "Who has hardened himself against Him and prospered?" (Job 9:4, NKJV) Job knew the answer and so do we: *nobody.* If we obey God's will, everything in life holds together; but if we disobey, everything starts to fall apart. Nowhere in the Bible is this truth better illustrated than in the experiences of Elimelech and his wife Naomi.

We see in this chapter three mistakes that we must avoid as we deal with the problems and trials of life.

1. Unbelief: trying to run from our problems (Ruth 1:1-5)
The time. Life was not easy in those days; for during the period of the Judges, "there was no king in Israel; but every man did what was right in his own eyes" (Jud. 17:6; and see 18:11; 19:1; 21:25). The Book of Judges is the story of Israel at one of its lowest points in history and is a record of division, cruelty, apostasy, civil war, and national disgrace. Spiritually speaking, we are living *today* in the Book of Judges; for there is no king in Israel, and there will not be until Jesus returns. Like Israel in the past, many of God's people today are living in unbelief and disobedience and are not enjoying the blessings of God.

It seems incredible that this beautiful love story should take place at such a calamitous period in the nation's history, but is this not true today? Today we experience national and international perplexities, moral decay, and difficulties of every kind, and yet God loves this lost world and is seeking for a bride. In spite of alarms in the headlines and dangers on the streets, we can be sure that God still loves the world and wants to save lost sinners. When you know Jesus Christ as Savior and Lord, no matter how tough the times may be, you are part of a beautiful love story.

But the Book of Ruth is a *harvest* story as well as a *love* story. During this dark time in Israel's history, God was seeking a bride and *reaping a harvest.* To be sure, Israel was reaping the harvest of their disobedience (Gal. 6:7); but God was producing the fruit of the Spirit in the lives of Ruth and Naomi. Today, the Lord is seeking a harvest and calls us to share in His labors (John 4:34-48). The harvest today is white and ready, but the laborers are still few (Luke 10:2).

The place. How strange that there should be a famine in Bethlehem, which means "house of bread"! In the Old Testament, a famine was often an evidence of God's discipline because His people had sinned against Him (Lev. 26:18-20;

Deut. 28:15, 23-24). During the time of the Judges, Israel repeatedly turned from God and worshiped the idols of the heathen nations around them; and God had to discipline them (Jud. 2:10-19). The godly had to suffer because of the ungodly, even in Bethlehem.

The decision. When trouble comes to our lives, we can do one of three things: endure it, escape it, or enlist it. If we only endure our trials, then trials become our master, and we have a tendency to become hard and bitter. If we try to escape our trials, then we will probably miss the purposes God wants to achieve in our lives. But if we learn to enlist our trials, they will become our servants instead of our masters and work for us; and God will work all things together for our good and His glory (Rom. 8:28).

Elimelech made the wrong decision when he decided to leave home. What made this decision so wrong?

He walked by sight and not by faith. Abraham made the same mistake when he encountered a famine in the land of promise (Gen. 12:10ff). Instead of waiting for God to tell him what to do next, he fled to Egypt and got into trouble. No matter how difficult our circumstances may be, the safest and best place is in the will of God. It's easy to say with David, "O that I had wings like a dove! I would fly away and be at rest" (Ps. 55:6). But it's wiser to claim the promise of Isaiah 40:31 and wait on the Lord for "wings like eagles" and by faith soar above the storms of life. *You can't run away from your problems.*

How do you walk by faith? By claiming the promises of God and obeying the Word of God, in spite of what you see, how you feel, or what may happen. It means committing yourself to the Lord and relying wholly on Him to meet the need. When we live by faith, it glorifies God, witnesses to a lost world, and builds Christian character into our lives. God has ordained that "the righteous will live by his faith" (Hab.

2:4; Rom. 1:17; Gal. 3:11; Heb. 10:38; 2 Cor. 5:7); and when we refuse to trust Him, we are calling God a liar and dishonoring Him.

There is a wisdom of this world that leads to folly and sorrow, and there is a wisdom from God that seems folly to the world but that leads to blessing (1 Cor. 3:18-20; James 3:13-18). "Woe unto them that are wise in their own eyes, and prudent in their own sight!" (Isa. 5:21, KJV)

He majored on the physical and not the spiritual. A husband and father certainly wants to provide for his wife and family, but he must not do it at the expense of losing the blessing of God. When Satan met Jesus in the wilderness, his first temptation was to suggest that Christ satisfy His hunger rather than please His Father (Matt. 4:1-4; see John 4:34). One of the devil's pet lies is: "You do have to live!" But it is *in God* that "we live and move and have our being" (Acts 17:28, NIV); and He is able to take care of us.

David's witness is worth considering: "I have been young, and now I am old; yet I have not seen the righteous forsaken, or his descendants begging bread" (Ps. 37:25, NKJV). As Paul faced a threatening future, he testified, "But none of these things move me, neither count I my life dear unto myself" (Acts 20:24, KJV). In times of difficulty, if we die to self and put God's will first (Matt. 6:33), we can be sure that He will either take us out of the trouble or bring us through.

He honored the enemy and not the Lord. By going fifty miles to the neighboring land of Moab, Elimelech and his family abandoned God's land and God's people for the land and people of the enemy. The Moabites were descendants of Lot from his incestuous union with his firstborn daughter (Gen. 19:30-38), and they were the Jews' enemies because of the way they had treated Israel during their pilgrim journey from Egypt to Canaan (Deut. 23:3-6; Num. 22–25). During the time of the Judges, Moab had invaded Israel and ruled over the people for eighteen years (Jud. 3:12-14); so why should Elimelech turn to them for help? They were a proud people (Isa. 16:6) whom God disdained. "Moab is My washpot," said the Lord (Ps. 60:8, KJV), a picture of a humiliated nation washing the feet of the conquering soldiers.

The consequences. The name Elimelech means "my God is king." But the Lord was *not* king in Elimelech's life, for he left God completely out of his decisions. He made a decision out of God's will when he went to Moab, and this led to another bad decision when his two sons married women of Moab. Mahlon married Ruth (Ruth 4:10), and Chilion married Orpah. Jews were forbidden to marry Gentile women, especially those from Ammon and Moab (Deut. 7:1-11; 23:3-6; Neh. 13:1-3; Ezra 9:1-4). It was the Moabite women in Moses' day who seduced the Jewish men into immorality and idolatry; and as a result, 24,000 people died (Num. 25).

Elimelech and his family had fled Judah to escape death, *but the three men met death just the same.* The family had planned only to "sojourn" temporarily in Moab, but they remained for ten years (Ruth 1:4). At the end of that decade of disobedience, all that remained were three lonely widows and three Jewish graves in a heathen land. Everything else was gone (v. 21). Such is the sad consequence of unbelief.

We can't run away from our problems. We can't avoid taking with us the basic cause of most of our problems, which is an unbelieving and disobedient heart. "The majority of us begin with the bigger problems outside and forget the one inside," wrote Oswald Chambers. "A man has to learn 'the plague of his own heart' before his own problems can be solved . . ." *(The Shadow of an Agony,* p. 76).

2. Deception: trying to hide our mistakes (Ruth 1:6-18)
We need to consider the three testimonies that are in this section.

17

The testimony of Naomi (Ruth 1:6-15). God visited His faithful people in Bethlehem, but not His disobedient daughter in Moab. Naomi heard the report that the famine had ended; and when she heard the good news, she decided to return home. There is always "bread enough and to spare" when you are in the Father's will (Luke 15:17, KJV). How sad it is when people only *hear* about God's blessing, but never experience it, because they are not in the place where God can bless them.

Many years ago, I was in a prayer meeting with a number of Youth for Christ leaders, among them Jacob Stam, brother of John Stam who, with his wife Betty, was martyred in China in 1934. We had been asking God to bless this ministry and that project, and I suppose the word "bless" was used scores of times as we prayed. Then Jacob Stam prayed, "Lord, we've asked you to bless all these things; but, please, Lord, *make us blessable."* Had Naomi been in that meeting, she would have had to confess, "Lord, I'm not blessable."

Whenever we have disobeyed the Lord and departed from His will, we must confess our sin and return to the place of blessing. Abraham had to leave Egypt and go back to the altar he had abandoned (Gen. 13:1-4), and Jacob had to go back to Bethel (35:1). The repeated plea of the prophets to God's people was that they *turn* from their sins and *return* to the Lord. "Let the wicked forsake his way, and the unrighteous man his thoughts, and let him return to the Lord, and He will have compassion on him; and to our God, for He will abundantly pardon" (Isa. 55:7).

Naomi's decision was right, but her motive was wrong. She was still interested primarily in food, not in fellowship with God. You don't hear her confessing her sins to God and asking Him to forgive her. She was returning to her land but not to her Lord.

But something else was wrong in the way Naomi handled

this decision: *She did not want her two daughters-in-law to go with her.* If it was right for Naomi to go to Bethlehem, where the true and living God was worshiped, then it was right for Orpah and Ruth to accompany her. Naomi should have said to them what Moses said to his father-in-law, "Come thou with us, and we will do thee good; for the Lord has spoken good concerning Israel" (Num. 10:29, KJV). Instead, Naomi tried to influence the two women to go back to their families and their false gods.

Why would a believing Jewess, a daughter of Abraham, encourage two pagan women to worship false gods? I may be wrong, but I get the impression that Naomi didn't want to take Orpah and Ruth to Bethlehem *because they were living proof that she and her husband had permitted their two sons to marry women from outside the covenant nation.* In other words, Naomi was trying to cover up her disobedience. If she returned to Bethlehem alone, nobody would know that the family had broken the Law of Moses.

"He who covers his sins will not prosper, but whoever confesses and forsakes them will have mercy" (Prov. 28:13, NKJV). When we try to cover our sins, it's proof that we really haven't faced them honestly and judged them according to God's Word. True repentance involves honest confession and a brokenness within. "The sacrifices of God are a broken spirit; a broken and a contrite heart, O God, Thou wilt not despise" (Ps. 51:17). Instead of brokenness, Naomi had bitterness.

The tragedy is that Naomi did not present the God of Israel in a positive way. In Ruth 1:13, she suggests that God was to blame for the sorrow and pain the three women had experienced. "It is more bitter for me than for you, because the Lord's hand has gone out against me!" (v. 13, NIV) In other words, "I'm to blame for all our trials, so why remain with me? Who knows what the Lord may do to me next?" Had

Naomi been walking with the Lord, she could have won Orpah to the faith and brought two trophies of grace home to Bethlehem.

The testimony of Orpah (Ruth 1:11-14). The two daughters-in-law started off with Naomi (v. 7), but she stopped them and urged them not to accompany her. She even prayed for them (vv. 8-9) that the Lord would be kind to them and find them new husbands and give them rest after all their sorrow. But of what value are the prayers of a backslidden believer? (Ps. 66:18) Three times Naomi told Orpah and Ruth to return (Ruth 1:8, 11-12).

When she saw them hesitating, Naomi began to reason with them. "I'm too old to have another husband and bear another family," she said. "And even if I could bear more sons, do you want to waste these next years waiting for them to grow up? You could be in your mother's house, with your family, enjoying life."

Orpah was the weaker of the two sisters-in-law. She started to Bethlehem with Naomi, kissed her, and wept with her; yet she would not stay with her. She was "not far from the kingdom" (Mark 12:34, NIV), but she made the wrong decision and turned back. Orpah kissed her mother-in-law, but we wonder whether her heart was really in it; for her decision proved that her heart was back home where she hoped to find a husband. Orpah left the scene and is never mentioned again in the Scriptures.

The testimony of Ruth (Ruth 1:15-18). Naomi was trying to cover up; Orpah had given up, but Ruth was prepared to stand up! She refused to listen to her mother-in-law's pleas or follow her sister-in-law's bad example. Why? *Because she had come to trust in the God of Israel (2:12).* She had experienced trials and disappointments, but instead of blaming God, she had trusted Him and was not ashamed to confess her faith. In spite of the bad example of her disobedient in-laws,

Ruth had come to know the true and living God; and she wanted to be with His people and dwell in His land.

Ruth's conversion is evidence of the sovereign grace of God, for the only way sinners can be saved is by grace (Eph. 2:8-10). Everything within her and around her presented obstacles to her faith, and yet she trusted the God of Israel. Her background was against her, for she was from Moab where they worshiped the god Chemosh (Num. 21:29; 1 Kings 11:7, 33), who accepted human sacrifices (2 Kings 3:26-27) and encouraged immorality (Num. 25). Her circumstances were against her and could have made her bitter against the God of Israel. First, her father-in-law died, and then her husband and her brother-in-law; and she was left a widow without any support. If this is the way Jehovah God treats His people, why follow Him?

Ruth dearly loved her mother-in-law, but even Naomi was against her; for she urged Ruth to return to her family and her gods in Moab. Since Elimelech and Mahlon were now dead, Ruth was technically under the guardianship of Naomi; and she should have obeyed her mother-in-law's counsel. But God intervened and graciously saved Ruth in spite of all these obstacles. "Not by works of righteousness which we have done, but according to His mercy He saved us" (Titus 3:5, NKJV). God delights in showing mercy (Micah 7:18), and often He shows His mercy to the least likely people in the least likely places. This is the sovereign grace of the God "who will have all men to be saved, and to come unto the knowledge of the truth" (1 Tim. 2:4, KJV).

Ruth's statement in Ruth 1:16-17 is one of the most magnificent confessions found anywhere in Scripture. First, she confessed her love for Naomi and her desire to stay with her mother-in-law even unto death. Then she confessed her faith in the true and living God and her decision to worship Him alone. She was willing to forsake father and mother (2:11) in order to cleave to Naomi and the God of her people. Ruth was steadfastly "determined" to accompany Naomi (1:18) and live in Bethlehem with God's covenant people.

But there was a divine law that said, "An Ammonite or Moabite shall not enter the congregation of the Lord; even to the tenth generation none of his descendants shall enter the congregation of the Lord forever" (Deut. 23:3, NKJV). This meant permanent exclusion. How then could Ruth enter into the congregation of the Lord? By trusting God's grace and throwing herself completely on His mercy. Law excludes us from God's family, but grace includes us if we put our faith in Christ.

When you read the genealogy of Jesus Christ in Matthew 4, you find the names of five women, four of whom have very questionable credentials: Tamar committed incest with her father-in-law (Gen. 38:3); Rahab was a Gentile harlot (Josh. 2:5); Ruth was an outcast Gentile Moabitess (Ruth 1:5); and "the wife of Uriah" was an adulteress (2 Sam. 11:6). How did they ever become a part of the family of the Messiah? Through the sovereign grace and mercy of God! God is "long-suffering toward us, not willing that any should perish but that all should come to repentance" (2 Peter 3:9, NKJV). (Mary is the fifth woman in the genealogy, and she was included because of God's grace and her faith. See Luke 1:26-56.)

3. Bitterness: blaming God for our trials (Ruth 1:19-22)

The two widows probably visited the three graves of their loved ones for the last time before leaving Moab. Then they committed themselves to the Lord and set out to begin a new life. It would be interesting to know what Naomi and Ruth talked about as they journeyed from Moab to Bethlehem. Did Naomi give her daughter-in-law some basic instruction in the Law of Moses? Did Ruth ask questions about the Jewish faith, the Jewish people, and her new home in Bethlehem? We wonder what kind of answers Naomi would have given since she was a bitter woman with a faltering faith in the God of Israel.

Naomi had been away from home for ten years, and the women of the town were shocked when they saw her. (In v. 19, the pronoun of "they said" is feminine.) Their question "Is this Naomi?" suggests both surprise and bewilderment. The name Naomi means "pleasant," but she was not living up to her name. She was not the Naomi whom they had known a decade before. Her ten difficult years in Moab, and the sorrows they had brought, had taken their toll on Naomi's appearance and personality. Instead of making her better, the trials of life had made her bitter, which is the meaning of the word *mara.*

We can't control the circumstances of life, but we can control how we respond to them. That's what faith is all about, daring to believe that God is working everything for our good even when we don't feel like it or see it happening. "In everything give thanks" (1 Thes. 5:18) isn't always easy to obey, but obeying this command is the best antidote against a bitter and critical spirit. The Scottish preacher George H. Morrison said, "Nine-tenths of our unhappiness is selfishness, and is an insult cast in the face of God." Because Naomi was imprisoned by selfishness, she was bitter against God.

To begin with, she accused the Lord of dealing very bitterly with her (Ruth 1:20). She had left Bethlehem with a husband and two sons and had come home without them. She had gone to Moab possessing the necessities of life, but now she had returned home having nothing. She was a woman with empty hands, an empty home, and an empty heart. Because she didn't surrender to the Lord and accept His loving chastening, she did not experience "the peaceful fruit of righteousness" (Heb. 12:11).

Not only had the Lord dealt bitterly with her, but He had also testified against her in these afflictions (Ruth 1:21). Is this Naomi's confession of sin, her admission that she and her family had sinned in going to Moab? Is she hinting that they deserved all that they had suffered? Twice Naomi called God "the Almighty," which is the Hebrew name El Shaddai, "the All-powerful One" (vv. 20-21). It's one thing to *know* God's name and quite something else to *trust* that name and allow God to work in the difficult situations of life. "And those who know Your name will put their trust in You; for You, Lord, have not forsaken those who seek You" (Ps. 9:10, NKJV). Naomi knew the name but did not exercise the faith.

But was Naomi really that poor and empty? Or was she simply exaggerating her situation because she was weary of body and bitter of soul? Just think of the resources she had that should have encouraged her.

For one thing, she had *life;* and this in itself is a precious gift from God—a gift we too often take for granted. Naomi left three graves back in Moab, but God in His goodness had kept her alive and brought her back to Bethlehem. "Fear not that your life shall come to an end," said John Henry Newman, "but rather that it shall never have a beginning." Naomi thought that life had ended for her, but her trials were really a new beginning. Naomi's faith and hope were about to die, but God had other plans for her!

Naomi not only had life, but she also had *opportunity.* She was surrounded by friends, all of whom wanted the very best for her. At first, her sorrow and bitterness isolated her from the community, but gradually that changed. Instead of sitting looking gloomily at a wall, she finally decided to look out the window; and then she got up and opened the door! When the night is the darkest, if we look up, we can still see the stars.

One of Naomi's richest resources was *her daughter-in-law Ruth.* In fact, it is Ruth whom God used and blessed throughout the rest of this book; for Ruth was a woman who trusted God and was totally committed to Him. Naomi soon learned that God's hand of blessing was on this young woman and that He would accomplish great things through her obedience.

But most of all, Naomi still had *Jehovah, the God of Israel.* The Lord is mentioned about twenty-five times in this brief book, for He is the Chief Actor in this drama whether Naomi realized it or not. "I firmly believe in Divine Providence," said President Woodrow Wilson. "Without it, I think I should go crazy. Without God the world would be a maze without a clue." When we fear God, we need not fear anything else. On his deathbed, John Wesley said, "Best of all, God is with us!" God is not only *with* us, but He is also *for* us; and "if God be for us, who can be against us?" (Rom. 8:31, KJV)

It was barley harvest when the two widows arrived in Bethlehem, a time when the community expressed joy and praise to God for His goodness. It was spring, a time of new life and new beginning. Alexander Whyte often told his Edinburgh congregation that the victorious Christian life is "a series of new beginnings," and he was right. Naomi was about to make a new beginning; for with God, it's never too late to start over again.

Are you trusting God for *your* new beginning? After all, with God at your side, your resources are far greater than your burdens.

Stop staring at the wall and, by faith, get up and open the door to a brand-new tomorrow.

The Greatest of These

(In which Boaz is surprised by love,
and Ruth is overwhelmed by grace)

Before God changes our circumstances, He wants to change our hearts. If our circumstances change for the better, but we remain the same, then we will become worse. God's purpose in providence is not to make us comfortable, but to make us conformable, "conformed to the image of His Son" (Rom. 8:29). Christlike character is the divine goal for each of His children.

Naomi was bitter against God, but Ruth was willing for God to have His way in her life; so God began His gracious work with Ruth. Ruth would influence Naomi, and then God would bring to pass a wonderful work that would eventually bring the Son of God into the world. Ruth and Naomi had no idea that they were part of an eternal plan that would fulfill God's promise to Abraham that his seed would bring blessing to the whole world (Gen. 12:1-3). Ruth's story begins with the death of a husband, but it will end with the birth of a baby. Her tears will be turned into triumph.

If we want God to work in our lives and circumstances and accomplish His gracious purposes, then there are certain conditions that we must meet. These conditions are illustrated in Ruth's experiences in this chapter.

1. We must live by faith in the Lord (Ruth 2:1-3)

A Latin proverb says, "Providence assists not the idle." Since Ruth was not the kind of woman who could long remain idle, she asked Naomi's permission to glean in the fields so they would have food to eat. This was a step of faith on Ruth's part, based on God's commandment in the Law (Lev. 19:9-10; 23:22; Deut. 24:19-22). Whenever they reaped a harvest, God's people were to consider the poor and leave gleanings for them. After all, God gave the harvest; and He had every right to tell the people how to use it.

The existence of this law was proof of God's concern for the poor among His people. The nation was instructed to treat the poor with equity (Ex. 23:3, 6; Lev. 19:15; Prov. 22:22-23) and with generosity (Lev. 19:9-10). God was also concerned for the widows, many of whom were poor, and He told the people to care for them (Ex. 22:22-24; see Isa. 10:1-2). Ruth was not only a poor widow, but she was also an alien. Therefore, she had every right to look to God for His help and provision. "He defends the cause of the fatherless and the widow, and loves the alien, giving him food and clothing" (Deut. 10:18, NIV).

To live by faith means to take God at His word and then act upon it, for "faith without works is dead" (James 2:20, NKJV). Since Ruth believed that God loved her and would provide for her, she set out to find a field in which she could glean. This was completely an act of faith because, being a stranger, she didn't know who owned the various parcels of ground that made up the fields. There were boundary markers for each parcel, but no fences or family name signs as seen on our farms today. Furthermore, as a woman and an outsider, she was especially vulnerable; and she had to be careful where she went.

It is here that Boaz enters the story (Ruth 2:1, 3), a relative of Elimelech who was "a man of standing" (NIV) in the community. His name means "in him is strength." By the providence of God, Ruth gleaned in the portion of the field that belonged to Boaz. The record says Ruth "happened" to come to this portion of the field, but it was no accident. Her steps were guided by the Lord. "I being in the way, the Lord led me" (Gen. 24:27, KJV).

God's providential working in our lives is both a delight and a mystery. God is constantly working *with us* (Mark 16:20), *in us* (Phil. 2:12-13), and *for us* (Rom. 8:28) and accomplishing His gracious purposes. We pray, we seek His will, and we make decisions (and sometimes make mistakes); but it is God who orders events and guides His willing children. In a spectacular vision, the Prophet Ezekiel saw the providential workings of God depicted by a throne set on a "firmament" that was moved here and there by "wheels within wheels" (Ezek. 1). You can't explain it, but thank God you can believe it and rely on it!

2. We must live by the grace of God (Ruth 2:4-16)

When Ruth set out that morning to glean in the fields, she was looking for someone who would show her grace (v. 2, and see vv. 10 and 13). Grace is favor bestowed on someone who doesn't deserve it and can't earn it. As a woman, a poor widow, and an alien, Ruth could have no claims on anyone. She was at the lowest rung of the social ladder.

The channel of that grace was Boaz. How good it is to know that God has good people living in bad times! If you knew only the record in the Book of Judges, you might conclude that the righteous had perished from the earth (Ps. 12:1-2; Isa. 57:1; 1 Kings 19:10; Micah 7:2). But there were still people like Boaz who knew the Lord and sought to obey His will. Boaz was concerned about his workers and wanted them to enjoy the blessing of the Lord (Ruth 2:4).

No sooner had Boaz greeted his workers than his eye

caught the presence of a stranger in the field, and a lovely stranger at that. I get the impression that when he saw her, it was love at first sight; for from that point on, Boaz focuses his interest on Ruth and not on the harvest. Though an alien, Ruth was an eligible young woman whom the young men of the town would notice (3:10). Ruth 2:11 indicates that Boaz had already heard about Ruth, but now he was about to meet her personally.

Again, we marvel at the overruling providence of God. The Lord led Ruth to the field of Boaz and then led Boaz to visit his field while Ruth was there. When Boaz arrived, Ruth might have been resting in the shelter house that Boaz provided for his workers; or she might have grown weary and gone home to Naomi. When we commit our lives to the Lord, what happens to us happens by way of appointment and not by accident. Ruth was still a poor widow and an alien, but God was about to create a new relationship that would completely alter her circumstances.

Bible students have seen in Boaz a picture of our Lord Jesus Christ in His relationship to His bride, the church. Like Ruth, the lost sinner is outside the covenant family of God, bankrupt, with no claim on God's mercy. But God took the initiative and provided a way for us to enter His family through faith in Jesus Christ. (See Eph. 2:10-22.) I will have more to say about this relationship when we get to the next chapter and we consider the "kinsman redeemer."

Now let's notice the evidences of God's grace in the way Boaz related to Ruth:

(1) Boaz took the initiative (Ruth 2:8). Grace means that God makes the first move to come to our aid, not because we deserve anything, but because He loves us and wants us for Himself. "We love, because He first loved us" (1 John 4:19, NKJV). God took the initiative in salvation when we were spiritually dead (Eph. 2:1-10), without strength (Rom. 5:6),

sinners (5:8), and His enemies (5:10). Salvation was not an afterthought of God but that which He planned from eternity. We have every reason to believe Boaz loved Ruth and therefore took the first steps to meet her needs.

(2) Boaz spoke to Ruth (Ruth 2:8). It was he who first spoke to her, for she would not have dared to speak to a man, especially one who was a stranger and "the lord of the harvest." What right did a widow and an alien have to address a great man like Boaz? Yet he interrupted his conversation with his foreman to speak to a poor stranger gleaning in his field.

Several years ago, my wife, younger daughter, and I visited Great Britain and found ourselves in Lichfield, where we learned that Queen Elizabeth was coming to dedicate a new school for exceptional children. We interrupted our plans and stood on the curb, waiting patiently for the motorcade, which finally appeared. We stood perhaps ten feet from the Queen as she slowly rode by with her lady-in-waiting, waving to the crowd in her distinctive manner.

Now, suppose she had rolled down the window and called, "Hello, Warren! Hello, Betty and Judy! I'll tell my guards to take care of you!" If that had happened, everybody would have been duly impressed with our importance and perhaps asked for our autographs. Imagine, here are three American citizens to whom the Queen speaks personally!

Queen Elizabeth has never spoken to me, and probably never will; *but Almighty God has spoken to me in Jesus Christ and through His Word!* "God . . . has in these last days spoken to us by His Son" (Heb. 1:1-2, NKJV). In spite of all that a world of sinners has done to the Lord, He still speaks to us in His grace. He not only speaks the word of salvation, but He also gives us the guidance we need for everyday life. Just as Boaz instructed Ruth, so the Lord also shares His Word of wisdom to direct our daily lives. He is the "Lord of the harvest" and assigns to us our place in His field.

(3) Boaz promised to protect Ruth and provide for her needs (Ruth 2:9, 14-16). Boaz called Ruth "my daughter" because she was younger than he (see 3:10), but it was also a term of endearment. He would treat her like a member of his family. (This is what David did for Mephibosheth. See 2 Sam. 9.) Boaz instructed his young men to protect her and the young women to work with her. She was to walk with the female servants who followed immediately after the reapers. In other words, Ruth had first chance at the best of the gleanings! Boaz even instructed his workers to allow her to glean among the sheaves and told them to deliberately drop some of the harvest so she could pick it up. If she was hungry or thirsty, she could refresh herself with his workers. In fact, Boaz ate with her and personally handed her the food! (Ruth 2:14)

What a picture of the grace of God! The master became like the servants that he might show his love to a foreigner. Ruth had no idea that Boaz had commanded his workers to be generous to her, but she believed his word and found that her needs were met. Jesus Christ came to this earth as a servant (Phil. 2:1-11) that He might save us and make us a part of His family. He has shared with us the riches of His mercy and love (Eph. 2:4), the riches of His grace (v. 7), the riches of His wisdom and knowledge (Rom. 11:33), His riches in glory (Phil. 4:19), and yes, His "unsearchable riches" (Eph. 3:8, NIV). We, undeserving "foreigners," are members of the family of God and have all of His inheritance at our disposal.

(4) Boaz encouraged Ruth (Ruth 2:10-13). Ruth's response to Boaz was one of humility and gratitude. She acknowledged her own unworthiness and accepted his grace. She believed his promises and rejoiced in them. There was no need for Ruth to worry, for the wealthy lord of the harvest would care for her and Naomi. How did she *know* he would care for her?

He gave her his promise, and she knew he could be trusted.

Ruth neither looked back at her tragic past nor did she look at herself and consider her sorry plight. She fell at the feet of the master and submitted herself to him. She looked away from her poverty and focused on his riches. She forgot her fears and rested on his promises. What an example for God's people today to follow!

I find that many people are miserable because they don't obey the admonition of Hebrews 12:2: "fixing our eyes on Jesus." They spend so much time looking at themselves, their circumstances, and other people that they fail to do what Ruth did, namely, center their attention on their Master. Instead of resting in His perfections, they focus on their own imperfections. Instead of seeing His spiritual riches, they complain about their bankruptcy. They go to church "to get their needs met," instead of going to church to worship the God who is greater than any need. They need to heed the counsel of the little poem a radio listener sent me years ago:

> Look at self and be distressed,
> Look at others and be depressed,
> Look at Jesus and you'll be blessed!

(5) Boaz saw to it that she was satisfied (Ruth 2:14, 18). All of this happened to Ruth because of her faith in the God of Israel. Boaz fully knew Ruth's story, for it didn't take long for news to travel in a little town like Bethlehem. He knew that Ruth had abandoned her home and her gods and had put her faith in Jehovah. She had taken refuge "under His wings." That image sometimes refers to the hen protecting her chicks (Ps. 91:4; Matt. 23:37), but it can also refer to the wings of the cherubim in the holy of holies (Pss. 36:7; 61:4). Ruth was no longer a foreigner and a stranger. She was not only accepted by the God of Israel, but she was also dwelling

in the very holy of holies with Him! (See Eph. 2:11-22.)

The word translated "answered" in Ruth 2:11 is literally "raised his voice." Boaz was getting excited! He wanted everybody to hear what he thought about Ruth, and he wasn't ashamed to be identified with her. She had trusted Jehovah, and she had proved her faith by cleaving to her mother-in-law and becoming a part of the people of Israel in Bethlehem. The phrase "spoken friendly" in verse 13 means "spoken to the heart." The Word of God comes from the heart of God (Ps. 33:11) to the hearts of His people (Matt. 23:18-23) and gives encouragement and hope (Rom. 15:4). If you listen to the voices of the world, you will be discouraged; but if you listen to the voice of God from His Word, your heart will be encouraged.

The Word of God and the Son of God can fully satisfy the heart of the believer. When we seek for satisfaction anywhere else, we will find ourselves disobedient and dissatisfied. The lost world labors for that which doesn't satisfy (Isa. 55:2), but the believer has full satisfaction because of the grace of the Lord Jesus Christ (Pss. 36:7-9; 63:5; 65:4; 103:5; 107:9). As the hymn writer put it:

> Well of water ever springing,
> Bread of life so rich and free,
> Untold wealth that never faileth,
> My Redeemer is to me.
> Hallelujah! I have found Him
> Whom my soul so long has craved!
> Jesus satisfies my longings,
> Through His blood I now am saved.
>
> (Clara T. Williams)

We must live by faith, and we must depend on God's grace. But there is a third condition we must meet.

3. We must live in hope (Ruth 2:17-23)

All day long, Ruth labored with a happy and hopeful heart. She didn't have to worry about the men harassing her or the other workers hindering her. She had food when she was hungry, drink when she was thirsty, and a place of rest when she became weary. The grain she gleaned amounted to about half a bushel, enough food for the two women for nearly a week. She also had some food left over from her lunch (v. 18). Ruth was not only a diligent worker, but she was also careful not to waste anything God had given her.

How will Naomi respond to Ruth's experiences? The last time we met Naomi, she was sharing her bitterness with the women of Bethlehem and blaming God for her sorrow and poverty. When Ruth had asked permission to go to the fields to glean, all Naomi said to her was "Go, my daughter" (v. 2). She gave her daughter-in-law no word of encouragement, not even the promise of her prayers.

But now we hear a new word from Naomi's lips — "Blessed!" (vv. 19-20) She not only blessed Ruth's benefactor, but she also blessed the Lord! We have moved from bitterness to blessedness. When Naomi saw the grain, she blessed the man who allowed Ruth to work in his field; and when she heard that the man was Boaz, Naomi blessed the Lord. What a change has taken place in the heart of this grieving widow! This change came about because of the new hope she had in her heart, and the one who gave her that new hope was Boaz.

Naomi had hope because of *who Boaz was* — a near kinsman who was wealthy and influential. As we shall see, a near kinsman could rescue relatives from poverty and give them a new beginning (Lev. 25:25-34). But she also had hope because of *what Boaz did:* He showed kindness to Ruth and took a personal interest in her situation. When Ruth shared with Naomi *what Boaz had said,* Naomi's hope grew even stronger because the words of Boaz revealed his love for

Ruth and his desire to make her happy. That Boaz insisted on Ruth staying close to his servants and in his field was proof to Naomi that her husband's relative was making plans that included her and her daughter-in-law.

Should not we who believe in Jesus Christ rejoice in hope? When you consider who He is, what He has done for us, and what He says to us in His Word, there is no reason for us to feel hopeless. Jesus Christ is the Son of God. He has died for us, and now He intercedes for us in heaven. In His Word, He has given us "exceeding great and precious promises" (2 Peter 1:4, KJV) that can never fail. No matter how you may feel today, no matter how difficult your circumstances may be, you can rejoice in hope if you will focus your faith on Jesus Christ.

The American agnostic lecturer Robert G. Ingersoll called hope "the only universal liar who never loses his reputation for veracity." But the late Norman Cousins, former editor of *The Saturday Review,* who miraculously survived an almost incurable illness and a severe heart attack, unequivocally disagrees with Ingersoll. "The human body experiences a powerful gravitational pull in the direction of hope," Cousins wrote. "That's why the patient's hopes are the physician's secret weapon. They are the hidden ingredients in any prescription." In his work with patients at the UCLA School of Medicine, Cousins proved the power of hope to change people's lives.

For the Christian believer, hope is not a shallow "hope-so feeling" generated by optimistic fantasies. Hope is an inner sense of joyful assurance and confidence as we trust God's promises and face the future with His help. This hope is God's gift to His children through the Holy Spirit, who reminds us of God's promises found in His Word (Rom. 15:13).

Ruth's half bushel of grain was the "firstfruits" of all that Boaz would do in the future, just as the Holy Spirit within us is the "firstfruits" of all that God has promised us (8:23). Although Ruth's supply of grain would be gone in a week, the witness of the Spirit within will remain until our hopes are all fulfilled when we see Jesus Christ.

The exciting new hope that now possessed the two widows was centered in a person, Boaz, just as our hope is centered in the Son of God. In fact, Jesus Christ *is* our hope (1 Tim. 1:1; 1 Thes. 1:3; Col. 1:27). Through faith in Christ, we have been born again into "a living hope" (1 Peter 1:3); and because it is a *living* hope, it grows stronger each day and produces fruit. The hopes that the world clings to are dead hopes, but ours is a living hope because it is rooted in the living Christ.

Naomi then explained to Ruth the law of "the kinsman redeemer" (Lev. 25:47-55). It was not just the kindness and love of Boaz for Ruth that gave Naomi confidence, for those wonderful feelings could change overnight. It was the principle of redemption that God had written in His Word that gave Naomi the assurance that Boaz would rescue them. As a near relative, Boaz could redeem the family property that Elimelech had mortgaged when he took his family to Moab. Naomi wasn't wealthy enough to redeem it, but Boaz could buy it back and keep it in the family.

However, something else was involved: The wife of the deceased went with the property. Therefore, the kinsman redeemer had to marry her and bring up children bearing the name of the deceased. They would then inherit the property, and the family name and family possessions would continue to be theirs. This is known as "levirate marriage" (see Deut. 25:5-10). The word *levir* is Latin for "a husband's brother." The author of the Book of Ruth doesn't explain how Ruth's husband Mahlon (4:10) was connected with his father's property so that Ruth had to be included in the purchase. When and why the Jewish people connected the law of the kinsman redeemer with the law of levirate marriage is not made clear to us, but that was the custom in Ruth's time.

Naomi cautioned Ruth to obey the commands of Boaz and stay close to his servants as she gleaned in the field. The barley harvest occurred during March and April, and the wheat harvest during June and July. Meanwhile, Ruth kept busy and gathered food sufficient for herself and her mother-in-law. But now she was laboring motivated by a wonderful hope: She was joyfully anticipating the day of redemption! (See Rom. 8:23 and Eph. 4:30.)

It is encouraging to see the changes that have taken place in Naomi because of what Ruth did. God used Ruth to turn Naomi's bitterness into gratitude, her unbelief into faith, and her despair into hope. One person, trusting the Lord and obeying His will, can change a situation from defeat to victory.

Ruth's faith in God's Word led her to the field of Boaz. The love of Boaz for Ruth compelled him to pour out his grace upon her and meet her every need. (Grace is love that pays the price to help the undeserving one.) Ruth's experience of grace gave her new hope as she anticipated what her kins-man redeemer would do.

"And now abide faith, hope, love" (1 Cor. 13:13), and they still abide with us as we abide in Jesus Christ and trust in Him.

THREE

The Midnight Meeting

(In which a simple act of faith
brings the dawning of a new day)

Ever since Boaz came into Ruth's life, Naomi has been a different person. Her concern is no longer for herself and her grief but for Ruth and her future. *It's when we serve others that we ourselves receive the greatest joy and satisfaction.* The martyred German minister Dietrich Bonhoeffer called Jesus Christ "the man for others," and the title is appropriate. "Be humble, thinking of others as better than yourself. Don't just think about your own affairs, but be interested in others, too, and in what they are doing" (Phil. 2:3-4, TLB).

When the two widows came to Bethlehem, their plan was that Ruth take care of Naomi and both of them eke out an existence the best they could. But now Naomi has a new plan: Ruth is to marry Boaz, and then all of them can live happily ever after. Naomi could tell from Ruth's report that Boaz would be in favor of the plan, so she began to set things in motion. In that day, it was the parents who arranged marriages; so Naomi was not out of place in what she did.

Keep in mind that the Book of Ruth is much more than the record of the marriage of a rejected alien to a respected Jew. It's also the picture of Christ's relationship to those who trust Him and belong to Him. In the steps that Ruth takes, recorded in this chapter, we see the steps God's people must take if they want to enter into a deeper relationship with the Lord. Like Ruth, we must not be satisfied merely with living on leftovers (2:2), or even receiving gifts (2:14, 16). *We must want Him alone; for when we have Him, we also have all that He owns.* It's not the gifts that we seek, but the Giver.

1. Ruth prepared to meet Boaz (Ruth 3:1-5)

There were other men who would gladly have married Ruth (v. 10), but they could not have redeemed her. Only a kinsman could do that, and Boaz was that kinsman. Since Naomi knew that Boaz would be using the threshing floor that night and staying there to guard his grain, she instructed Ruth to prepare herself to meet him. Ruth made a fivefold preparation before she presented herself to Boaz.

First, *she washed herself (v. 3a).* Every day in the United States, 450 billion gallons of water are used for homes, factories, and farms, enough water to cover Manhattan to a depth of ninety-six feet. In the East, the heat and the dust made frequent washing a necessity; but water was not always plentiful. With regard to the Jews, the Law of Moses required ceremonial washings, and taking a bath and changing clothes usually preceded a special event (Gen. 35:1-3). Actually, Naomi was telling Ruth to act like a bride preparing for her wedding (Ezek. 16:9-12).

If we want to enter into a deeper relationship with our Lord, we must "cleanse ourselves from all filthiness of the flesh and spirit, perfecting holiness in the fear of God" (2 Cor. 7:1, NKJV). Whenever we sin, we must pray, "Wash me" (Ps. 51:2, 7); but sometimes God says to us, "Wash yourselves, make yourselves clean" (Isa. 1:16, NKJV). When we seek forgiveness, God washes the record clean (1 John 1:9); but God will not do for us what we must do for ourselves. Only we can put out of our lives those things that defile us, *and we*

40

know what they are. It might mean cleaning out our library (Acts 19:18-20), our cassette and CD collection, the magazine rack, or perhaps the TV viewing schedule. We must separate ourselves from whatever defiles us and grieves the Father (2 Cor. 6:14–7:1; James 4:7-8).

If the Old Testament priests came into God's presence defiled, they were in danger of death (Ex. 30:17-21). The Jewish people were conscious of the need for holiness as they came to worship God (Pss. 15; 24:1-6); yet Christians today rush into God's presence without cleansing themselves of the sins that rob them of God's blessing. Is it any wonder that our worship is often an empty routine and that the power of God doesn't come to our meetings?

The next thing Ruth did to prepare was to *anoint herself (Ruth 3:3b).* Eastern peoples used fragrant oils to protect and heal their bodies and to make themselves pleasant to others. A bride would especially take care to wear fragrant perfume that would make her "nice to be near" (see Song 1:3, 12-14; 4:11-16).

Anointing oil speaks of the presence and the working of the Holy Spirit in our lives. All believers have received the anointing of the Spirit (1 John 2:20, 27), and therefore we ought to be "a fragrance of Christ" to the Heavenly Father (2 Cor. 2:15). The more we are like Jesus Christ in character and conduct, the more we please our Father; and the more we please Him, the more He can bless and use us for His glory.

I once heard Dr. A.W. Tozer say, "If God were to take the Holy Spirit out of this world, much of what the church is doing would go right on; and nobody would know the difference." We have so much in human resources available to the church today that we manage to "serve the Lord" without the unction of the Holy Spirit working in our lives. But is that what God wants?

41

While here on earth, Jesus lived His life and did His work through the anointing of the Holy Spirit (Luke 4:16-19). If the spotless Son of God needed the Spirit's power, how much more do we! Do we dare pray in the energy of the flesh when the Spirit is present to assist us? (Rom. 8:26; Eph. 2:18) Do we try to witness for Christ without asking the Spirit to help us? (Acts 1:8) Can we fellowship with our Lord in His Word apart from the ministry of the Spirit of God? (Eph. 1:15-23 and 3:14-21)

Ruth's third act of preparation was to *change clothes (Ruth 3:3c)*. She was to put off the garments of a sorrowing widow and dress for a wedding (see Isa. 61:1-3). Ruth probably didn't have a large wardrobe, but she would have one special garment for festive occasions. Naomi had the faith to believe that Ruth would soon be going to a wedding!

In Scripture, clothing carries a spiritual meaning. After they had sinned against God, our first parents tried to cover themselves; but only the Lord could forgive them and clothe them acceptably, and He had to shed blood to do it (Gen. 3:1-8, 21). The Jewish priests wore special garments that nobody else was permitted to wear (Ex. 28). Salvation is pictured as a change of clothes (Luke 15:22; Isa. 61:10), and Christian living means taking off the "graveclothes" of the old life and putting on the "grace clothes" of the new life (Col. 3:1-17; see John 11:44).

We can't come into God's presence in our own righteousness, for "all our righteousnesses are as filthy rags" (Isa. 64:6, KJV). We can only come in the righteousness of Jesus Christ (2 Cor. 5:21), for we are "accepted in the beloved" (Eph. 1:6, KJV). If we are obedient to His will and seek to please Him, then our garments will be white (Rev. 19:8); but if we've sinned, we must confess our sins and seek His cleansing (Zech. 3). If you want to enter into a deeper fellowship with your Lord, then "let your garments always be white, and let your head lack no oil" (Ecc. 9:8, KJV).

Ruth prepared herself to meet Boaz *by learning how to present herself to him (Ruth 3:3-4).* There was nothing improper about this procedure, for it was the only way Ruth could offer herself to her kinsman redeemer. She had to put herself at the feet of the lord of the harvest, and he would do the rest.

Suppose that on her way to the threshing floor, Ruth decided to take a different approach. Why lie at the feet of the man you want to marry? Why uncover his feet and then ask him to put a corner of his mantle over you? Certainly there ought to be a better way! Had she used another approach, Boaz would have been confused; and the entire enterprise would have failed.

The Old Testament priests knew how to approach God because He gave them their instructions in the law. New Testament Christians know how to approach God because in the Word He has told us what is required. Whether in our private communion with the Lord or in public worship, we have no right to alter the principles of approach that God has laid down.

While ministering one week near Springfield, Illinois, my wife and I decided to visit the Abraham Lincoln house. In order to get in, we each had to have a ticket that could be procured at only one place. We had to follow the guide and not deviate from the route of the tour. Last but not least, we had to deposit our chewing gum in a container outside the house! If we wanted to see Mr. Lincoln's house, we had to conform to the rules.

Like the Prodigal Son (Luke 15:11-24), lost sinners can come to the Lord just as they are; and He will receive them and change them. But God's own children must "conform to the rules" if they want to fellowship with their Father (Heb. 10:19-25). When the people of God assemble for worship, we

43

must be careful to worship Him "in spirit and in truth" (John 4:24), following the principles given in the Scriptures. When it comes to worshiping God, too often people do that which is right in their own eyes and substitute human inventions for divine instructions.

Finally, *Ruth promised to obey (Ruth 3:5)*. "All that you say to me I will do" (NKJV). She was not only a hearer of the Word, but she was a doer. A willingness to obey the Lord is the secret of knowing what He wants us to do and being blessed when we do it. "If anyone is willing to do God's will, he shall know concerning the teaching" (John 7:17, literal translation). The will of God is not a cafeteria where we can pick and choose what we want. God expects us to accept *all* that He plans for us and to obey Him completely. Coming to God with a hidden agenda and with reservations in our hearts will only lead to grieving the Spirit and missing God's best.

2. Ruth submitted to Boaz (Ruth 3:6-9)

The harvest season was an especially joyful time for the Jews (Isa. 9:3; 16:10), which is the way God wanted it. "The Lord thy God shall bless thee in all thine increase, and in all the works of thine hands, therefore thou shalt surely rejoice" (Deut. 16:15, KJV). Most people today live separated from the sources of their daily bread and don't realize all that's involved in producing food. Perhaps our table prayers would be more joyful and more grateful if we realized all that a farmer goes through to help keep us alive.

Harvesting and threshing were cooperative enterprises. The men of a village would take turns using the threshing floor, which was usually a raised platform outside the village and often on a hill where it could catch the evening breeze. The men would deposit the sheaves on the floor and then separate the grain from the stalks by having oxen walk on it (Deut. 25:4) or by beating the stalks (see Ruth 2:17). Once the grain was separated, the workers would throw the grain into the air; and the breeze would carry the chaff away while the grain fell to the floor. The grain would then be heaped up to be carried away for marketing or storage. The men often worked in the evening when the breeze was up, and they slept at the threshing floor to protect the harvest.

Four times in this chapter there is mention of feet (3:4, 7-8, 14). Ruth had fallen at the feet of Boaz in response to his gracious words (2:10), but now she was coming to his feet to propose marriage. She was asking him to obey the law of the kinsman redeemer and take her as his wife.

We may ask, "Why didn't Ruth wait for Boaz to propose to her?" His statement in 3:10 suggests the first reason: He fully expected that she would marry one of the younger bachelors in Bethlehem. Boaz was an older man, and Ruth was a young woman (4:12). Evidently he concluded that he was out of the running. But the most important reason is given in verse 12: There was a nearer kinsman in town who had first option on Ruth and the property, and Boaz was waiting for him to act. Ruth had forced the issue, and now Boaz could approach this kinsman and get him to decide.

"Life is full of rude awakenings!" a famous cartoon canine likes to say, and more than one biblical character would agree. Adam went to sleep and woke up to discover he'd been through surgery and was now a married man. Jacob woke up to discover he was married to the wrong woman! Boaz woke up at midnight to find a woman lying at his feet.

When he asked who she was, Ruth replied that she was Ruth; but she did not call herself "the Moabitess." Now she was the "handmaid" of Boaz. She was making a new beginning. You find Ruth named twelve times in this little book, and in five of these references she is identified with Moab (1:22; 2:2, 21; 4:5, 10).

To spread one's mantle over a person meant to claim that

person for yourself (Ezek. 16:8; 1 Kings 19:19), particularly in marriage. The word translated "skirt" also means "wing." Ruth had come under the wings of Jehovah God (Ruth 2:12); and now she would be under the wings of Boaz, her beloved husband. What a beautiful picture of marriage!

3. Ruth listened to Boaz (Ruth 3:10-14)

In the responses of Boaz to Ruth, we see how the Lord responds to us when we seek to have a deeper fellowship with Him. Just as Boaz spoke to Ruth, so God speaks to us from His Word.

He accepts us (Ruth 3:8-10). Boaz might have refused to have anything to do with Ruth; but in his love for her, he accepted her. He even called her "my daughter" (see 2:8) and pronounced a blessing on her (see Eph. 1:3). Our Heavenly Father and our Redeemer are seeking for a closer relationship with us, and we should not be afraid to draw near and share Their love (John 14:21-24; James 4:7-8). If we could only realize in even a small way the great love our Kinsman Redeemer has for us, we would forsake everything else and enjoy His fellowship.

He assures us (Ruth 3:11-13). In the midnight darkness, Ruth couldn't see the face of Boaz, but she could hear his voice; and that voice spoke loving assurance to her: "Fear not!" *Our assurance is not in our feelings or our circumstances but in His Word.*

> How firm a foundation, ye saints of the Lord,
> Is laid for your faith in His excellent Word.

During the Boxer Rebellion, when the workers with the China Inland Mission were experiencing great suffering, the founder James Hudson Taylor, then in his late seventies, said to some colleagues, "I cannot read; I cannot think; I cannot even pray; but I can trust." "So then faith comes by hearing, and hearing by the word of God" (Rom. 10:17, NKJV).

"Fear not" is the word of assurance that the Lord gave to many of His servants: to Abraham (Gen. 15:1), Isaac (26:24), Jacob (46:3), Moses and the nation of Israel (Ex. 14:13), Joshua (Josh. 8:1; 10:8), King Jehoshaphat (2 Chron. 20:17), the Jewish remnant returning to their land (Isa. 41:10, 13-14; 43:1, 5; 44:2), the Prophet Ezekiel (Ezek. 3:9), the Prophet Daniel (Dan. 10:12, 19), Joseph (Matt. 1:20), Zacharias (Luke 1:13), Mary (1:30), the shepherds (2:10), Paul (Acts 27:24), and the Apostle John (Rev. 1:17). You and I can say with these spiritual giants, "The Lord is my helper; I will not fear" (Heb. 13:6, NKJV).

Not only did Boaz calm Ruth's fears, but he also made a promise to her concerning the future: "I will do for you all that you request" (Ruth 3:11, NKJV). Whatever God starts, He finishes; and what He does, He does well (Phil. 1:6; Mark 7:37). It was not Ruth's obligation to do for herself what only Boaz could do.

What seemed to Naomi to be a simple procedure has now turned out to be a bit more complicated, because there was a man in Bethlehem who was a nearer kinsman. Boaz didn't withhold this problem from Ruth, for he didn't want her to return home with false hopes in her heart. Joy and peace that are based on ignorance of the true facts are but delusions that lead to disappointments. The great concern of Boaz was the redemption of Ruth, even if another kinsman redeemer had to do it.

When you see this as a picture of our redemption in Jesus Christ, it impresses you strongly that *God obeyed His own law when He accomplished our salvation in Christ.* His law said, "The soul who sins shall die" (Ezek. 18:4, NKJV), and God didn't seek for some way to evade this. "He who did not spare His own Son, but delivered Him up for us all" (Rom.

8:32). Of course, there was no other "kinsman" who could redeem a lost world. "Neither is there salvation in any other: for there is none other name under heaven given among men, whereby we must be saved" (Acts 4:12, KJV).

4. Ruth received gifts from Boaz (Ruth 3:15-17)

During her days as a gleaner, Ruth had received generous treatment from Boaz. His workers had allowed her to follow the harvesters; they protected her from harm; they deliberately dropped sheaves for her to pick up. Boaz had shared the noon meal with Ruth, even handing her the parched grain with his own hands (2:14). On that first day of gleaning, Ruth had gone home with a little more than half a bushel of grain; but now Boaz filled her cloak with two bushels of grain, which would be more than two weeks' supply.

Boaz not only calmed Ruth's fears and gave her assurance for the future, but he also met her present needs in a gracious and generous way. She had not asked him for anything, but he gave the grain to her because he loved her. He was about to marry her, and he didn't want his prospective bride gleaning in the fields like a poor laborer.

Naomi's question in 3:16 has puzzled translators and interpreters. Why would her own mother-in-law ask her who she was? *The Living Bible* paraphrases the question, "Well, what happened, dear?" and both the NIV and the NASB read, "How did it go, my daughter?" But the *Authorized Version* translates the Hebrew text as it stands: "Who are you, my daughter?" In other words, "Are you still Ruth the Moabitess, *or are you the prospective Mrs. Boaz?*"

Ruth remembered Boaz's words, as she had done before (2:19-21); and she shared with Naomi all that Boaz had promised. Then Ruth showed Naomi the generous gift Boaz had given them. A man who sends a generous gift to his prospective mother-in-law is certainly a good choice for a husband!

Naomi could no longer say that her hands were empty (1:21). Now they were full because of the grace of the kinsman redeemer. Ruth's faith and obedience had brought about a complete transformation in their lives, and now they were living by grace.

5. Ruth waited for Boaz to work (Ruth 3:18)

It is "through faith and patience" that we inherit the promises (Heb. 6:12; 10:36). Since Naomi and Ruth believed that Boaz would accomplish what he said he would do, they waited patiently until they received the good news that Ruth would be a bride. "Commit your way to the Lord, trust also in Him, and He will do it" (Ps. 37:5).

I confess that *waiting* is one of the most difficult things for me to do, whether it's waiting for a table at a restaurant or waiting for a delayed flight to take off. I'm an activist by nature, and I like to see things happen on time. Perhaps that's why the Lord has often arranged for me to wait. During those times, three phrases from Scripture have encouraged me: "Sit still" (Ruth 3:18, KJV), "Stand still" (Ex. 14:13, KJV), and "Be still" (Ps. 46:10, KJV).

"Sit still" was Naomi's counsel to Ruth, and wise counsel it was. Ruth would have accomplished nothing by following Boaz around Bethlehem, trying to help him keep his promises. "Their strength is to sit still" (Isa. 30:7, KJV). Our human nature gets nervous and wants to help God out; and when we try, we only make matters worse.

"Stand still" was the command of Moses to the people of Israel when the Egyptian army was pursuing them. There was no need to panic, for God had the situation well in hand. Then the Lord commanded the people to "go forward" (Ex. 14:15), and He led them safely through the sea. There is a time to stand and a time to march, and we must be alert to know which one God wants us to do.

49

"Be still, and know that I am God" (Ps. 46:10, KJV) is a wonderful antidote for a restless spirit. The Hebrew word translated "be still" means "take your hands off, relax." It's so easy for us to get impatient with the Lord and start meddling in matters that we ought to leave alone. He is God, and His hands can accomplish the impossible. Our hands may get in the way and make matters worse.

Boaz was busy working for Ruth, and Naomi was confident that he wouldn't rest until he had settled the matter. "Being confident of this very thing, that He which hath begun a good work in you will perform [complete] it until the day of Jesus Christ" (Phil. 1:6, KJV). It encourages my heart to know that Jesus Christ is working unceasingly *for* His people as He intercedes in heaven (Heb. 8:34), and that He is working *in* us, seeking to conform us to His perfect will (13:20-21; Phil. 2:12-13).

Have you put yourself at the feet of the Lord of the Harvest, and are you trusting Him to work?

One evidence of your trust will be your willingness to sit still and let Him have His way.

Love Finds a Way

(In which Boaz and Ruth get married, and Naomi finds her empty heart full of joy and her empty hands full of a baby boy)

The Book of Ruth opens with three funerals but closes with a wedding. There is a good deal of weeping recorded in the first chapter, but the last chapter records an overflowing of joy in the little town of Bethlehem. "Weeping may endure for a night, but joy cometh in the morning" (Ps. 30:5, KJV). Not all of life's stories have this kind of happy ending; but this little book reminds us that, for the Christian, *God still writes the last chapter.* We don't have to be afraid of the future.

This chapter focuses on three persons: a bridegroom, a bride, and a baby.

1. The bridegroom (Ruth 4:1-10)

The law of the kinsman redeemer is given in Leviticus 25:23-34, and the law governing levirate marriage is found in Deuteronomy 25:5-10. The purpose of these laws was to preserve the name and protect the property of families in Israel. God owned the land and didn't want it exploited by rich people who would take advantage of poor people and widows. When obeyed, these laws made sure that a dead man's family name did not die with him and that his property was not sold outside the tribe or clan. The tragedy is that the Jewish rulers didn't always obey this law, and the prophets had to rebuke them for stealing land from the helpless (1 Kings 21; Isa. 5:8-10; Hab. 2:9-12). The nation's abuse of the land was one cause for their Captivity (2 Chron. 36:21).

The meaning of redemption. The word *redeem* means "to set free by paying a price." In the case of Ruth and Naomi, Elimelech's property had either been sold or was under some kind of mortgage, and the rights to the land had passed to Ruth's husband Mahlon when Elimelech died. This explains why Ruth was also involved in the transaction. She was too poor, however, to redeem the land.

When it comes to *spiritual* redemption, all people are in bondage to sin and Satan (Eph. 2:1-3; John 8:33-34) and are unable to set themselves free. Jesus Christ gave His life as a ransom for sinners (Mark 10:45; Rev. 5:9-10), and faith in Him sets the captive free.

Each time I visit a bookstore, I try to observe what subjects are getting prominent notice; and in recent years, it's been the theme of *deliverance.* I see shelves of books about addiction and codependence and how to find freedom. In a world that's enjoying more political freedom than ever before, millions of people are in bondage to food, sex, drugs, alcohol, gambling, work, and dozens of other "masters." While we thank God for the help counselors and therapists can give, it is Jesus Christ who alone can give freedom to those who are enslaved. "Therefore if the Son makes you free, you shall be free indeed" (John 8:36, NKJV).

The marks of the redeemer. Not everybody could perform the duties of a kinsman redeemer. To begin with, *he had to be a near kinsman (Lev. 25:25).* This was the major obstacle Boaz had to overcome because another man in Bethlehem was a nearer relative to Ruth than he was (3:12-13). When you see this as a type of Jesus Christ, it reminds you that He had to become *related* to us before He could redeem us. He became flesh and blood so He could die for us on the cross (Heb. 2:14-15). When He was born into this world in human flesh, He became our "near kinsman"; and He will remain our "kinsman" for all eternity. What matchless love!

In order to qualify, the kinsman redeemer also *had to be able to pay the redemption price.* Ruth and Naomi were too poor to redeem themselves, but Boaz had all the resources necessary to set them free. When it comes to the redemption of sinners, nobody but Jesus Christ is rich enough to pay the price. Indeed, the payment of money can never set sinners free; it is the shedding of the precious blood of Christ that has accomplished redemption (1 Peter 1:18-19; see Ps. 49:5-9). We have redemption through Christ's blood (Eph. 1:7), because He gave Himself for us (Titus 2:14) and purchased eternal redemption for us (Heb. 9:12).

There was a third qualification: The kinsman redeemer *had to be willing to redeem.* As we shall see in this chapter, since the nearer kinsman was not willing to redeem Ruth, Boaz was free to purchase both the property and a wife. The nearer kinsman had the money but not the motivation: He was afraid he would jeopardize his own family's inheritance.

The method of redemption. In ancient times, the city gate was the official court where judicial business was transacted in the presence of the elders (Deut. 21:18-21; 2 Sam. 15:2; Job 29:7ff). When Boaz arrived at the gate, he gathered ten men to witness the transaction. Just then, the nearer kinsman walked by—another evidence of God's providence—and Boaz hailed him. Now everything was ready for the great transaction that would ultimately involve the coming of the Son of God into the world.

The key theme of this chapter is *redemption.* The words "redeem," "buy," and "purchase" are used at least fifteen times. *There can be no redemption without the paying of a price.* From our point of view, salvation is free to "whosoever shall call on the name of the Lord" (Acts 2:21, KJV); but from God's point of view, redemption is a very costly thing.

The other kinsman was willing to buy the land until he learned that Ruth was a part of the transaction, and then he backed out. His explanation was that, in marrying Ruth, he would jeopardize his own inheritance. If he had a son by Ruth, and that son were his only surviving heir, Mahlon's property *and part of his own estate* would go to Elimelech's family. The fact that Ruth was a Moabitess may also have been a problem to him. (Both Mahlon and Chilion had married Moabite women and died!)

Boaz was undoubtedly relieved when his relative stepped aside and opened the way for Ruth to become his wife. It's worth noting that the nearer kinsman tried to protect his name and inheritance; *but we don't even know what his name was or what happened to his family!* Boaz took the risk of love and obedience, and his name is written down in Scripture and held in honor. "He who does the will of God abides forever" (1 John 2:17, NKJV). This also explains why Orpah's name is missing in Ruth 4:9-10.

The custom of taking off the shoe probably relates to the divine commandment to walk on the land and take possession (Gen. 13:17; Deut. 11:24; Josh. 1:3). In years to come, the ten witnesses would be able to testify that the transaction had been completed because they saw the kinsman hand his shoe to Boaz. It symbolized the kinsman's forfeiture of his right to possess the land. Boaz now had the land—and Ruth!

I have mentioned before that Boaz is a picture of Jesus Christ, our Kinsman Redeemer; and this scene is no exception to that. Like Boaz, Jesus wasn't concerned about jeopardizing His own inheritance; instead, He made us a part of His inheritance (Eph. 1:11, 18). Like Boaz, Jesus made His plans privately, but He paid the price publicly; and like Boaz, Jesus did what He did because of His love for His bride.

However, there are also some contrasts between Boaz and the Lord Jesus Christ. Boaz purchased Ruth by giving out of his wealth, while Jesus purchased His bride by giving Himself on the cross. Boaz didn't have to suffer and die to get a bride. Boaz had a rival in the other kinsman, but there was no rival to challenge Jesus Christ. Boaz took Ruth that he might raise up the name of the dead (Ruth 4:10), but we Christians glorify the name of the living Christ. There were witnesses on earth to testify that Ruth belonged to Boaz (vv. 9-10), but God's people have witnesses from heaven, the Spirit, and the Word (1 John 5:9-13).

Five times in Ruth 4:1-2 you find people *sitting down.* When Jesus Christ finished purchasing His bride, He sat down in heaven (Heb. 1:3; Mark 16:19) because the transaction was completed. "It is finished!"

2. The bride (Ruth 4:11-12)

It's a wonderful thing when the covenant community sincerely rejoices with the bride and groom because what they are doing is in the will of God. In my pastoral ministry, I've participated in a few weddings that were anything but joyful. We felt like grieving instead of celebrating. The popular entertainer George Jessel defined marriage as "a mistake every man should make," but the last place you want to make a mistake is at the marriage altar. Contrary to what some people believe, marriage is not "a private affair." This sacred union includes God and God's people, and every bride and groom should want the blessing of God and God's people on their marriage.

The people prayed that Ruth would be fruitful in bearing children, for in Israel children were considered a blessing and not a burden (Ps. 127:3-5). Alas, that's not the attitude in society today. In the United States each year, a million and a half babies are legally destroyed in the womb, and the pieces of their bodies removed as though they were cancerous tumors. A Christian nurse said to me one day, "In one part of our hospital, we're working day and night to keep little babies alive. In another part, we're murdering them. What is God going to say?"

It was important that the Jewish wives bear children, not only to perpetuate the nation, but also because it would be through Israel that God would send the Messiah to earth. The Jews abhorred both abortion and the exposing of children to die—practices that were common in other nations. Jacob's two wives, Leah and Rachel, bore to him eight sons who "built" the nation by founding the leading tribes of Israel (Gen. 29:31–30:24; 35:18). The use of the word *Ephrathah* in Ruth 4:11 is significant, for the Hebrew word means "fruitful." The people wanted Ruth to be fruitful and famous and bring honor to their little town. It was the place where Rachel was buried (Gen. 35:19), but more importantly, it would be known as the place where Jesus Christ was born.

The neighbors also wanted the house of Boaz to be like that of Perez (Ruth 4:12; see Matt. 1:3). The family of Perez had settled in Bethlehem (1 Chron. 2:5, 50-54), and Boaz was a descendant of Perez (v. 18). Tamar, the mother of Perez, was not a godly woman; but her name is found in our Lord's genealogy (Matt. 1:3).

What wonderful changes came into Ruth's life because she trusted Boaz and let him work on her behalf! She went from loneliness to love, from toil to rest, from poverty to wealth, from worry to assurance, and from despair to hope. She was no longer "Ruth the Moabitess," for the past was gone, and she was making a new beginning. She was now "Ruth the wife of Boaz," a name she was proud to bear.

One of the many images of the church in the Bible is "the bride of Christ." In Ephesians 5:22-33, the emphasis is on Christ's love for the church as seen in His ministries: He died for the church (past), He cleanses and nourishes the church through the Word (present), and He will one day present the church in glory (future). Christ is preparing a beautiful home for His bride and one day will celebrate His wedding (Rev. 19:1-10; 21–22).

3. The baby (Ruth 4:13-22)

God had been gracious to Ruth back in Moab by giving her the faith to trust Him and be saved. His grace continued when she moved to Bethlehem, for He guided her to the field of Boaz where Boaz fell in love with her. God's grace continued at the town gate where the nearer kinsman rejected Ruth and Boaz purchased her. After the marriage, God poured out His grace on Ruth and Boaz by giving her conception (Gen. 29:31; 30:1-2; 33:5) and then by giving her the safe delivery of a son, whom they named Obed ("servant").

God would use this baby to be a source of blessing to many.

Obed was a blessing to Boaz and Ruth. This was no ordinary baby, for it was God's special gift to Boaz and Ruth; and what a blessing little Obed was to their home! But *every* baby is a special gift from God and should be treated that way. Every baby deserves a loving home and caring parents who want to raise the child "in the training and admonition of the Lord" (Eph. 6:4, NKJV). What a great privilege it is to bring new life into the world and then to guide that life so it matures to become all that God has planned!

Obed was also a blessing to Naomi. His grandmother informally "adopted" him as her own son and became his foster mother. The women of Bethlehem shared Naomi's joy when they said, "Praise be to the Lord, who this day has not left you without a kinsman-redeemer" (Ruth 4:14, NIV). The reference is to Obed, not Boaz.

Obed was a "restorer of life" to Naomi. Every grandparent

can bear witness that grandchildren are better than the Fountain of Youth, for we "get young again" when the grandchildren come to visit. Though not all grandparents agree with it, they all know the saying: "They're called 'grandchildren' because they're grand when they come and grand when they leave." *There's no better way to get a new lease on life than to start investing yourself in the younger generation.* Every baby that is born into this world is a vote for the future, and grandparents need to focus on the future and not on the past. When you're holding a baby, you're holding the future in your arms.

Obed would be a blessing to Naomi in another way: He would one day care for the family that brought him into the world, including his grandmother Naomi. Boaz had redeemed the family inheritance; now Obed would continue the family line, protect the inheritance, and use it to sustain Naomi. He would live up to his name and be a "servant" to Naomi, his "foster mother."

The guarantee for this ministry would not be the law of the land but the love of Ruth for her mother-in-law. Obed would early learn to love Naomi even as Ruth loved her. Obed was an only son, but his affection for his mother and grandmother would be equal to that of seven sons.

Obed would bring blessing to Bethlehem. The child would bring fame to both the family name and the name of his native town. Elimelech's name almost disappeared from Israel, but Obed would make that name famous and bring glory to Bethlehem. This happened, of course, through the life and ministry of King David (v. 22) and of David's greater Son, Jesus Christ. Naomi would have the comfort of knowing that the family name would not perish but increase in fame.

Obed would bring blessing to Israel. Obed was the grandfather of King David, one of Israel's greatest rulers. When the name of David is mentioned, we usually think of either Goliath or Bathsheba. David did commit a great sin, but he was also a great man of faith whom God used to build the kingdom of Israel. He led the people in overcoming their enemies, expanding their inheritance and, most of all, worshiping their God. He wrote worship songs for the Levites to sing and devised musical instruments for them to play. He spent a lifetime gathering wealth for the building of the temple, and God gave him the plans for the temple so Solomon could do the job. Whether he had in his hand a sling or sword, a harp or hymnal, David was a great servant of God who brought untold blessings to Israel.

Obed would bring blessing to the whole world. The greatest thing God did for David was not to give him victory over his enemies or wealth for the building of the temple. The greatest privilege God gave him was that of being the ancestor of the Messiah. David wanted to build a house for God, but God told him He would build a house (family) for David (2 Sam. 7). David knew that the Messiah would come from the kingly tribe of Judah (Gen. 49:8-10), but nobody knew which family in Judah would be chosen. God chose David's family, and the Redeemer would be known as "the son of David" (Matt. 1:1).

Little did those Bethlehemites know that God had great plans for that little boy! Obed would have a son named Jesse; and Jesse would have eight sons, the youngest of which would be David the king (1 Sam. 16:6-13).[1] Remember that the next time you behold a baby or a child, that little one might be one for whom God has planned a great future. The medieval teacher who always tipped his hat to his pupils had the right idea, for among them perhaps was a future general or emperor.

---

[1] In 1 Chronicles 2:13-15, the writer states that Jesse had *seven* sons, but this is not an error or contradiction. The unnamed son must have died either unmarried or without posterity. Therefore, his name was dropped out of the official genealogy.

The Moabites were not to enter the congregation of the Lord "even to the tenth generation" (Deut. 23:3). But the little Book of Ruth closes with a ten-generation genealogy that climaxes with the name of David!

Never underestimate the power of the grace of God.

INTERLUDE:

REFLECTIONS ON RUTH

The main purpose of the Book of Ruth is historical. It explains the ancestry of David and builds a bridge between the time of the Judges and the period when God gave Israel a king.

But the Bible is more than a history book. There are many practical lessons to be learned from these events — lessons that can encourage us in our spiritual walk. The Book of Ruth is no exception.

This little book certainly reveals the providence of God in the way He guided Ruth and Naomi. It encourages me to know that God still cares for us even when we're bitter toward Him, as Naomi was. God directed Ruth, a "new believer," and used her faith and obedience to transform defeat into victory. God is concerned about the details of our lives, and this fact should give us courage and joy as we seek to live each day to please Him.

The Book of Ruth beautifully illustrates God's work of salvation. The story opens with Ruth as an outsider, a stranger, but it ends with Ruth as a member of the covenant community because she has married Boaz, her kinsman redeemer. He paid the price for her to be redeemed.

But the book also illustrates the believer's deepening relationship with the Lord. In chapter 1, Ruth doesn't even know that Boaz exists. In chapter 2, Ruth is a poor laborer, gleaning in the field of Boaz and receiving his gifts. To her, Boaz is only a mighty man of wealth who shows kindness to her. The turning point is in chapter 3 where Ruth yields herself at the feet of Boaz and believes his promises. The result is recorded in chapter 4: Ruth is no longer a poor gleaner, for now she has Boaz, *and everything he owns belongs to her.*

Too many of God's people are content to live in chapter 2, picking up the leftovers and doing the best they can in their difficult situation. They want God's gifts, but they don't want a deeper communion with God. What a difference it would make if they would only surrender themselves to the Lord and focus on the Giver instead of the gifts! Ponder John 14:21-24.

The Book of Ruth reminds us that God is at work in our world, seeking a bride and reaping a harvest; and we must find our place in His program of winning the lost. The events in the Book of Ruth occurred during the period of the Judges, a time not much different from our own day. If you focus only on the evils of our day, you'll become pessimistic and cynical; but, if you ask God what field He wants you to work in and faithfully serve Him, you'll experience His grace, love, and joy.

Judges is the book of "no king" (17:6; 18:1; 19:1; 21:25). First Samuel is the book of "man's king," when God gave Saul to Israel because they asked for him. Things will get so bad in our world that the nations will one day cry out for a king to feed them and protect them. That king will appear; and we call him the Antichrist.

But 1 Samuel isn't the end of the story, for 2 Samuel is the book of *God's king!* David did appear on the scene, and he did establish the kingdom in the name of the Lord. Likewise, when man's king has done his worst, God's King will appear, judge this evil world, put away ungodliness, and then establish His glorious kingdom.

Meanwhile, even though we must live in an evil time like the age of the Judges when there was no king in Israel, we can still seek first the kingdom of God and be loyal subjects of the King of kings (Matt. 6:33). The name Elimelech means "my God is king," but Elimelech didn't live up to his name, for he doubted God and disobeyed Him. Even though there is no king in Israel and all around us everything seems to be falling apart, there can be a King in our lives, reigning in our hearts.

It was Ruth's commitment that made the difference in her life and in the lives of the people she loved.

Have you put yourself at the feet of the Lord of the harvest? Until you do, God can never be to you all that He wants to be.

The Book of Esther

PRELUDE

When you turn from the Book of Ruth to the Book of Esther, you enter a new atmosphere. You go from a quiet little Jewish village to a bustling Gentile city, from doing business at the city gate to obeying the decrees of a sovereign monarch, from the joys of the simple life to the intrigues of a complex empire.

Ruth and Esther lived in different worlds, but the same God was present and at work in their lives, even though His name is not once mentioned in the Book of Esther. "While there is no name of God, and no mention of the Hebrew religion anywhere," wrote G. Campbell Morgan, "no one reads this book without being conscious of God" *(The Living Messages of the Books of the Bible,* vol. 1, p. 269). The God of the fields in the Book of Ruth is also the God of the feasts in the Book of Esther. He guides the poor gleaner in the harvest and overrules the powerful king on the throne. He has His way with both of them, though He never violates their freedom.

This fact ought to encourage God's people. Whether you live on a farm, in a small town, in the suburbs, or in a metropolis, God is there and is always at work on behalf of His people. Nobody can escape the watchful eye or the faithful hand of Almighty God, for God "works all things according to the counsel of His will" (Eph. 1:11, NKJV).

One of the major themes of this book is the providence of God. Kings may issue their unalterable decrees, but God overrules and accomplishes His purposes. When I was studying theology in seminary, I learned from Augustus Hopkins Strong's *Systematic Theology* that providence was "that continuous agency of God by which He makes all the events of

67

the physical and moral universe fulfill the original design with which He created it" (p. 419). Then Dr. Strong added this wonderful sentence: "Providence is God's attention concentrated everywhere" (p. 420). What an encouraging definition! "God's attention concentrated everywhere."

But why is God not mentioned in this book? The word "king" is found over 100 times in the Book of Esther, and the name of the king nearly 30 times; but God's glorious name is not mentioned once. (God's name is also absent from Song.) Is it because the Jewish nation was displeasing to God at that time and under His discipline? Perhaps. The events described in this book took place between 483 and 473 B.C. when the Persians were in control. The Book of Esther fits between chapters 6 and 7 of the Book of Ezra. Xerxes ruled from 485 to 465, and Esther became queen in 479. At that time a Jewish remnant was struggling to rebuild their nation in the Holy Land (Ezra 1–6), but the people were not totally committed to God.

This much is true: Though God is not named in this book, He is present and active. He was not *hiding;* He was only *hidden.* The Book of Esther is one of the greatest illustrations in the Bible of Romans 8:28. God faithfully works "according to His will in the army of heaven, and among the inhabitants of the earth" (Dan. 4:35, NKJV). This means that we can trust Him without fear and obey Him without hesitation; "for the kingdom is the Lord's: and He is the governor among the nations" (Ps. 22:28, KJV).

Why was the Book of Esther included in the Scriptures? For one thing, it explains the origin of the Jewish Feast of Purim. This is a joyful feast that our Jewish friends celebrate annually on the fourteenth and fifteenth days of March. Since this feast is not included in Leviticus 23, or anywhere else in the Law, its meaning would be a mystery to us were it not for the Book of Esther.

This book also reminds us that God was caring for His people Israel and fulfilling His promise to Abraham (Gen. 12:1-3). Every enemy that has ever tried to exterminate the Jewish nation has been defeated. At Passover, the Jews celebrate God's victory over Egypt. Every December at Hanukkah ("Feast of Lights"), they celebrate the victory of Judas Maccabaeus and the cleansing of the temple in Jerusalem. Purim commemorates their victory over Haman and his conspiracy in the Persian Empire. Satan continues to attack Israel, but the Jews, protected by God, are still in the community of nations and will be until Jesus comes and establishes them in their promised kingdom.

Many people today are so caught up in an impersonal mechanistic universe of scientific law that they forget what James Russell Lowell wrote in his famous poem "The Present Crisis":

> Careless seems the great Avenger;
>   history's pages but record
> One death-grapple in the darkness
>   'twixt old systems and the Word;
> Truth forever on the scaffold,
>   Wrong forever on the throne—
> Yet that scaffold sways the future,
>   and, behind the dim unknown,
> Standeth God within the shadow,
>   keeping watch above His own.

Finally, there is a powerful personal message in the Book of Esther; for Esther, like Ruth, is a beautiful example of a woman committed to God. Ruth's "Whither thou goest, I will go" (Ruth 1:16, KJV) is paralleled by Esther's "And if I perish, I perish" (Es. 4:16, KJV). Both women yielded themselves to the Lord and were used by God to accomplish great things.

Ruth became a part of God's wonderful plan for Israel to bring the Savior into the world, and Esther helped save the nation of Israel so that the Savior could be born.

God can use poor peasants and powerful queens to accomplish His divine purposes in this world. The question is not *"Where* do I live and work?" but *"For whom* do I live and work, for myself or my Lord?" Most of us are familiar with the famous statement of Socrates, "Know thyself." However, we need to get acquainted with a statement by Pittacus, one of the Seven Wise Men of Greece: "Know thine opportunities." God gave Esther the opportunity to surrender herself and serve Him and His people, and she seized that opportunity. Ambrose Bierce defined opportunity as "a favorable occasion for grasping a disappointment." Not so for the dedicated Christian! Opportunity is for us a favorable occasion for grasping *His appointment* and accomplishing His purposes.

We must never think that the days of great opportunities are all past. Today, God gives to His people many exciting opportunities to "make up the hedge, and stand in the gap" (Ezek. 22:30, KJV), if only we will commit ourselves to Him. Not only in your church, but in your home, your neighborhood, your place of employment, your school, even your sickroom, God can use you to influence others and accomplish His purposes, if only you are fully committed to Him.

A Suggested Outline of the Book of Esther

Theme: God's providence in protecting His people
Theme verses: 4:13-14

I. Esther's Coronation—chaps. 1–2
   1. The dethroning of Vashti—1
   2. The crowning of Esther—2

II. Haman's Condemnation—chaps. 3–7
   1. Haman's intrigue—3
   2. Mordecai's insight—4
   3. Esther's intercession—5–7

III. Israel's Celebration—chaps. 8–10
   1. A new decree—8
   2. A sure defense—9
   3. A great distinction—10

F I V E

The Queen Says, "No!"

(In which a family disagreement
grows into a national crisis)

L et's begin by getting acquainted with the king. His Persian name was Khshayarshan, which in Hebrew becomes
Ahasuerus and in the Greek language, Xerxes. His father was
Darius I, and his grandfather was Cyrus the Great; so he
came from an illustrious family. Ahasuerus ruled over the
Persian Empire from 486 to 465 B.C. The empire was divided
into twenty "satrapies," which in turn were subdivided into
"provinces"; and the king was in absolute control.

Like most monarchs of that day, Ahasuerus was a proud
man; and in this chapter, we see three evidences of his pride.

1. His boastfulness (Es. 1:1-9)
Eastern rulers enjoyed hosting lavish banquets because each
occasion gave them opportunity to impress their guests with
their royal power and wealth. Three banquets are mentioned
in this chapter: one for the key military and political officers
of the empire (vv. 1-4); one for the men of Shushan (Susa in
Greek), site of the king's winter palace (vv. 5-8); and one for
the women of Shushan (v. 9), presided over by Queen Vashti.

The king probably didn't assemble all his provincial leaders
at one time; that would have kept them away from their

duties for six months and weakened the empire. It's more likely that, over a period of six months, Ahasuerus brought the officers to Shushan on a rotating schedule. Then, having consulted with them, the king would bring them all together for the seven-day feast so they could confer collectively. In Esther 1:11, the writer indicates that the princes were also at this week-long festivity.

Along with these three banquets, at least six other feasts are recorded in this book: Esther's coronation banquet (2:18); Haman's celebration feast with the king (3:15); Esther's two banquets for Haman and the king (chaps. 5 and 7); the Jews' banquets when they heard the new decree (8:17); and the Feast of Purim (9:17-19). It's wonderful how God can accomplish His eternal purposes through such a familiar activity as people eating and drinking! (See 1 Cor. 10:31.)

What was the purpose behind the banquet for the nobles and officials of the empire? Scripture doesn't tell us, but secular history does. The Greek historian Herodotus (485–425 B.C.) may refer to these banquets in his *History*, where he states that Ahasuerus was conferring with his leaders about a possible invasion of Greece. Ahasuerus' father, Darius I, had invaded Greece and been shamefully defeated at Marathon in 490. While preparing to return to Greece and get revenge, Darius had died (486 B.C.); and now his son felt compelled to avenge his father and expand his empire at the same time. Herodotus claims that Ahasuerus planned to invade all of Europe and "reduce the whole earth into one empire."

According to Herodotus, the king's words were these: "My intent is to throw a bridge over the Hellespont and march an army through Europe against Greece, that thereby I may obtain vengeance from the Athenians for the wrongs committed by them against the Persians and against my father."[1]

---

[1]See Herodotus, *The History,* Book VII, section 8.

The king's uncle, Artabanus, strongly opposed the plan, but the king persisted and succeeded in convincing the princes and officers to follow him.

It was important that Ahasuerus impress his nobles and military leaders with his wealth and power. When they saw the marble pillars, the gorgeous drapes hung from silver rings, the gold and silver couches on beautiful marble mosaic pavements, and the golden table service, what else could they do but submit to the king. Like the salesperson who takes you out to an exclusive restaurant for an expensive dinner, the king broke down their resistance. A proud man himself, he knew how to appeal to the pride in others.

Unfortunately, this ostentatious display of wealth couldn't guarantee the Persians a military victory. In 480 B.C., the Persian navy was destroyed at Salamis, while the king sat on a throne watching the battle; and in 479 B.C., the Persian army was defeated at Plataea. Thus ended Ahasuerus' dream of a world empire. If ever a man should have learned the truth of Proverbs 16:18, it was Ahasuerus: "Pride goes before destruction, and a haughty spirit before a fall" (NKJV).

People in authority need to remember that all authority comes from God (Rom. 13:1) and that He alone is in complete control. Pharaoh had to learn that lesson in Egypt (Ex. 7:3-5); Nebuchadnezzar had to learn it in Babylon (Dan. 3-4); Belshazzar learned it at his blasphemous banquet (Dan. 5); Sennacherib learned it at the gates of Jerusalem (Isa. 36-37); and Herod Agrippa I learned it as he died, being eaten by worms (Acts 12:20-23). Every man or woman in a place of authority is second in command, for Jesus Christ is Lord of all.

2. His drunkenness (Es. 1:10-12)

Scripture ignores these military matters because the writer's purpose was to explain how Esther became queen. It was at the conclusion of the seven-day banquet that Ahasuerus, "in high spirits from wine" (Es. 1:10, NIV), ordered his queen to display her beauty to the assembled guests; but she refused to obey. Her response, of course, was a triple offense on her part. Here was a woman challenging the authority of a man, a wife disobeying the orders of her husband, and a subject defying the command of the king. As a result, "the king became furious and burned with anger" (v. 12, NIV).

As you study the Book of Esther, you will discover that this mighty monarch could control everything but himself. His advisers easily influenced him; he made impetuous decisions that he later regretted; and when he didn't get his own way, he became angry. Susceptible to flattery, he was master of a mighty empire but not master of himself. "He who is slow to anger is better than the mighty, and he who rules his spirit, than he who captures a city" (Prov. 16:32). Ahasuerus built a great citadel at Shushan, but he couldn't build his own character. "Whoever has no rule over his own spirit is like a city broken down, without walls" (25:28, NKJV). The king could control neither his temper nor his thirst.

This is a good place to stop and consider alcohol and anger—two powerful forces that have brought more destruction to our society than even the statistics reveal.

While we appreciate the king's wisdom in not forcing his guests to drink (Es. 1:8), we can hardly compliment him on the bad example he set by his own drinking habits. The Bible doesn't *command* total abstinence, but it does emphasize it. The nation of Israel didn't drink strong drink during their wilderness pilgrimage (Deut. 29:5-6), and the priests were instructed not to drink wine or strong drink while serving in the tabernacle (Lev. 10:8-11). The Nazirites were forbidden not only to drink wine but even to eat the skin or seeds of the grape (Lev. 6:1-3). Though our Lord Jesus drank wine while here on earth, He is today a "total abstainer." People who claim Jesus as their example in social drinking, and even

76

point out that He turned water into wine, should take Luke 22:18 into consideration: "For I say unto you, I will not drink of the fruit of the vine, until the kingdom of God shall come" (KJV). I wonder whether these people "follow His example" in any other areas of life, such as praying, serving, and sacrificing. (Probably not.)

Most of the advertisements that promote the sale of alcoholic beverages depict fashionable people in gracious settings, giving the subtle impression that "social drinking" and success are synonymous. But pastors, social workers, physicians, and dedicated members of Alcoholics Anonymous would paint a different picture. They've seen firsthand the wrecked marriages, ruined bodies and minds, abused families, and shattered careers that often accompany what people call "social drinking."

Longtime baseball coach and manager Connie Mack said that alcohol had no more place in the human body than sand had in the gas tank of an automobile. Alcohol is a narcotic, not a food; it destroys, not nourishes. The Bible warns against drunkenness (Prov. 20:1; 21:17; 23:20-21, 29-35; Isa. 5:11; Luke 21:34; Rom. 13:13-14; 1 Cor. 5:11; Eph. 5:18; 1 Peter 4:3-5); and even the *Koran* says, "There is a devil in every berry of the grape."

The best way to avoid drunkenness is not to drink at all. A Japanese proverb warns, "First the man takes a drink, then the drink takes a drink, and then the drink takes the man." And King Lemuel's mother taught him, "It is not for kings, O Lemuel, it is not for kings to drink wine; nor for princes strong drink" (Prov. 31:4, KJV).

As for the anger that King Ahasuerus expressed toward his lovely queen, it was ignorant, childish, and completely uncalled for. Had the king been sober, he would never have asked his wife to display her beauties before his drunken leaders. His pride got the best of him; for if he couldn't command his own wife, how could he ever command the Persian armies? Since Vashti had embarrassed the king before his own leaders, the king had to do something to save both his ego and his reputation.

Vashti was right, and Ahasuerus was wrong; and his anger was only further proof that he was wrong. Anger has a way of blinding our eyes and deadening our hearts to that which is good and noble. The Italian poet Pietro Aletino (1492–1557) wrote to a friend, "Angry men are blind and foolish, for reason at such a time takes flight and, in her absence, wrath plunders all the riches of the intellect, while the judgment remains the prisoner of its own pride." If anybody was a prisoner of pride, it was the exalted king of the Persian Empire!

To be sure, there's a holy anger against sin that ought to burn in the heart of every godly person (Rom. 12:9). Even our Lord manifested anger at sin (Mark 3:5), but we must be careful that our anger at sin doesn't become sinful anger (Eph. 4:26). Sometimes what we call "righteous indignation" is only unrighteous temper masquerading in religious garments. Jesus equated anger with murder (Matt. 5:21-26), and Paul warns us that anger can hinder our praying (1 Tim. 2:8).

Pride feeds anger, and as it grows, anger reinforces pride. "A quick-tempered man acts foolishly," warned the writer of Proverbs 14:17, a text perfectly illustrated by King Ahasuerus. Instead of being angry at Vashti, the king should have been angry at himself for acting so foolishly.

Before leaving this part of our story, I want to point out that the Gospel of Jesus Christ has helped to liberate and elevate women in society wherever it has been preached and obeyed throughout the world. "There is neither Jew nor Greek, there is neither bond nor free, there is neither male nor female: for ye are all one in Christ Jesus" (Gal. 3:28, KJV). We still have a long way to go in our recognition of the importance of women in the church, but thanks partly to the influence of the Gospel, society has made progress in setting women free from cruel bondage and giving them wonderful opportunities for life and service.[2]

3. His vindictiveness (Es. 1:13-22)

When the ego is pricked, it releases a powerful poison that makes people do all sorts of things they'd never do if they were humble and submitted to the Lord. Frances Bacon wrote in his *Essays*, "A man that studies revenge keeps his own wounds green, which otherwise would heal and do well." Had Ahasuerus sobered up and thought the matter through, he would never have deposed his wife. After all, she showed more character than he did.

The Persian king had seven counselors who advised him in matters of state and had the right to approach his throne. They also knew well how to flatter the king to secure their positions and get from him what they wanted. The phrase "understood the times" (v. 13) suggests that they were astrologers who consulted the stars and used other forms of divination. Eastern monarchs in that day depended on such men to give them instructions in matters personal, governmental, and military. (See Dan. 1:20; 2:2, 10, 17; 4:7; 5:7, 11, 17.)

Concerned about the repercussions of Vashti's disobedience, the king asked his seven counselors what he should do. The first thing they did was exaggerate the importance of the event: Vashti had done wrong not only to the king but also to the entire empire! Therefore, when the guests returned home, they would tell everybody that the queen was disobe-

---

[2]One of the best presentations on this subject is *Daughters of the Church*, by Ruth A. Tucker and Walter Liefeld (Zondervan, 1987). See also *A Dictionary of Women in Church History*, by Mary L. Hammack (Moody Press, 1984).

dient to her husband, and the consequences would be disastrous. The women in the empire would hold the men in contempt, and a general rebellion of wives against husbands and women against men would follow. (Commentators point out that the word "women" in Es. 1:17 means "women in general," while "ladies" in v. 18 refers to the women of the aristocratic class.) These counselors were playing it smart; for by exaggerating the problem, they also inflated their own importance and made the king more dependent on them.

But was the situation really that serious? When Vashti refused to obey, I wonder how many princes and nobles at the banquet said among themselves, "Well, the king's marriage is just like our marriages! His wife has a mind of her own, and it's a good thing she does!" It's doubtful that the king would have lost authority or stature throughout the empire had he shrugged his shoulders, smiled, and admitted that he'd done a foolish thing. "A fool shows his annoyance at once, but a prudent man overlooks an insult" (Prov. 12:16, NIV).

The seven wise men advised the king to depose Vashti and replace her with another queen. They promised that such an act would put fear in the hearts of all the women in the empire and generate more respect for their husbands. But would it? Are hearts changed because kings issue decrees or congresses and parliaments pass laws? How would the punishment of Vashti make the Persian women love their husbands more? Are love and respect qualities that can be generated in hearts by human fiat?

How could seven supposedly wise men be so calloused in their treatment of Vashti and so foolish in their evaluation of the women of the empire? How could they be so brutal as to use the authority of the law to destroy one woman and threaten the peace of every home in the empire? They were encouraging every husband to act like King Ahasuerus and manage the home on the basis of executive fiat (Es. 1:22). What a contrast to Paul's counsel to husbands and wives in Ephesians 5:18-33!

Still motivated by anger and revenge, and seeking to heal his wounded pride, the king agreed to their advice and had Vashti deposed (Es. 1:19-21). He sent his couriers throughout the empire to declare the royal edict—an edict that was unnecessary, unenforceable, and unchangeable. King Ahasuerus was given to issuing edicts, and he didn't always stop to think about what he was doing (3:9-12). It was another evidence of his pride.

The king didn't immediately replace Vashti. Instead, he went off to invade Greece, where he met with humiliating defeat; and when he returned home, he sought solace in satisfying his sensual appetite by searching for a new queen and filling his harem with candidates. The women in his empire were not only to be subservient to the men, but they were also to be "sex objects" to give them pleasure. The more you know about Ahasuerus and his philosophy of life, the more you detest him.

The Bible doesn't tell us what happened to Vashti. Many biblical scholars believe she was Amestris, the mother of Artaxerxes who ruled from 464 to 425 B.C. It's likely that Esther was either out of favor or dead; for Amestris exercised great influence as the queen mother during her son's reign.

Artaxerxes was born in 483, the year of the great banquet described in Esther 1. It's possible that Vashti was pregnant with her son at that time and therefore unwilling to appear before the men. It was her son Artaxerxes who ruled during the times of Ezra (7:1, 7, 11-12, 21; 8:1) and Nehemiah (2:1; 5:14; 13:6).

In any case the stage was now set for the entrance of the two key persons in the drama: Haman, the man who hated the Jews, and Esther, the woman who delivered her people.

The New Queen

(In which Esther becomes the king's wife,
and Mordecai gets no reward for saving the king's life)

God is preparing His heroes," said A.B. Simpson, founder of the Christian and Missionary Alliance, "and when the opportunity comes, He can fit them into their places in a moment, and the world will wonder where they came from."

Dr. Simpson might have added that God also prepares His *heroines,* for certainly Esther was divinely prepared for her role as the new queen. *God is never surprised by circumstances or at a loss for prepared servants.* He had Joseph ready in Egypt (Ps. 105:17), Ezekiel and Daniel in Babylon, and Nehemiah in Susa; and He had Esther ready for her ministry to the Jews in the Persian Empire.

As you read this chapter, you will see at least three evidences of the hand of God at work in the affairs of the people.

1. The agreement of the king (Es. 2:1-4)

Nearly four years have passed since Vashti was deposed. During that time, Ahasuerus directed his ill-fated Greek campaign and came home in humiliation instead of honor. As he considered his rash actions toward his wife, his affection for Vashti rekindled; and though he had a harem full of concubines, he missed his queen. There is a difference between love and sex. The passing excitement of the moment is not the same as the lasting enrichment of a lifetime relationship.

The king's advisers were concerned that Vashti not be restored to royal favor; for if she regained her throne, their own lives would be in danger. After all, it was they who had told the king to remove her! But more was involved than the lives of the king's counselors, for the survival of the Jewish nation was also at stake. Queen Vashti would certainly not intercede on behalf of the Jews. She probably would have cooperated with Haman.

Knowing the king's strong sensual appetite, the counselors suggested that he assemble a new harem composed of the most beautiful young virgins in the empire. This was not a "beauty contest" where the winners were rewarded by having a chance for the throne. These young women were conscripted against their will and made a part of the royal harem. Every night, the king had a new partner; and the next morning, she joined the rest of the concubines. The one that pleased the king the most would become his new queen. It sounds like something out of *The Arabian Nights,* except that, in those tales, Emperor Shahriar married a new wife each day and had her slain the next morning. That way he could be sure she wouldn't be unfaithful to him!

I wonder how many beautiful girls hid when the king's officers showed up to abduct them? Heartbroken mothers and fathers no doubt lied to the officers and denied that they had any virgin daughters. Perhaps some of the girls married any available man rather than spend a hopeless life shut up in the king's harem. Once they had been with the king, they belonged to him and could not marry. If the king ignored them, they were destined for a life of loneliness, shut up in a royal harem. Honor? Perhaps. Happiness? No!

"The king's heart is in the hand of the Lord, like the rivers of water; He turns it wherever He wishes" (Prov. 21:1, NKJV).

This doesn't mean that God forced Ahasuerus to accept the plan, or that God approved of the king's harems or of his sensual abuse of women. It simply means that, without being the author of their sin, God so directed the people in this situation that decisions were made that accomplished God's purposes.

The decisions made today in the high places of government and finance seem remote from the everyday lives of God's people, but they affect us and God's work in many ways. It's good to know that God is on His throne and that no decision is made that can thwart His purposes. "He does as He pleases with the powers of heaven and the peoples of the earth. No one can hold back His hand or say to Him: 'What have You done?' " (Dan. 4:35, NIV)

"There is no attribute of God more comforting to His children than the doctrine of divine sovereignty," said Charles Haddon Spurgeon. While we confess that many things involved in this doctrine are shrouded in mystery, it's unthinkable that Almighty God should not be Master of His own universe. Even in the affairs of a pagan empire, God is in control.

2. The choice of Esther (Es. 2:5-18)

We are now introduced to Mordecai and his cousin Esther, who, along with Haman, are the principal players in this drama. Once again, we see the hand of God at work in the life of this lovely Jewess. Consider the factors involved.

The influence of Mordecai (Es. 2:5-7). Mordecai is named fifty-eight times in this book, and seven times he is identified as "a Jew" (2:5; 5:13; 6:10; 8:7; 9:29, 31; 10:3). His ancestor, Kish, was among the Jews taken to Babylon from Jerusalem in the second deportation in 597 B.C. (2 Kings 24). Cyrus, King of Persia, entered Babylon in 539 and the next year gave the Jews permission to return to their land. About

85

50,000 responded (Ezra 1–2). In subsequent years, other Jews returned to Israel; but Mordecai chose to remain in the Persian capital.

While the Babylonians made life difficult for the Jews, the Persians were more lenient to aliens; and many Jews prospered in the land of their captors. Mordecai eventually held an official position in the government and sat at the king's gate (Es. 2:21). It's likely that he was given this position after Esther's coronation, because he had to walk back and forth in front of the house of the women in order to find out how his adopted daughter was doing (v. 11). If he were an officer of the king, he would have had access to inside information.

Esther was Mordecai's cousin and adopted daughter (v. 15). Her Persian name *Esther* means "star," and her Hebrew name *Hadassah* means "myrtle." (It's interesting that the myrtle tree bears a flower that looks like a star.) A beautiful woman, she was one of those taken into the king's harem. An English proverb says, "Beauty may have fair leaves, yet bitter fruit." We wonder how many young ladies in the empire regretted that they had been born beautiful!

One of the key elements in this story is the fact that the people in Shusan didn't know that Mordecai and Esther were Jews. The palace personnel found out about Mordecai when he told them (3:4), and the king learned about Esther at the second banquet she hosted for him and Haman (chap. 7).

This fact presents us with some problems. For one thing, if Mordecai and Esther were passing themselves off as Persians, they certainly weren't keeping a kosher home and obeying the laws of Moses. Had they been following even the dietary laws, let alone the rules for separation and worship, their true nationality would have quickly been discovered. Had Esther practiced her Jewish faith during her year of preparation (2:12), or during the four years she had been queen (2:16 with 3:7), the disguise would have come off.

Anyone has the right to conceal his or her true nationality, and this is not a sin. As long as nobody asked them, Mordecai and Esther had every right to conceal their racial origin. If people thought that the two cousins were Gentiles, well, that was their own conclusion. Nobody lied to them. "All truths are not to be spoken at all times," wrote Matthew Henry, "though an untruth is not to be spoken at any time." Nevertheless, that Esther and Mordecai did not acknowledge the God of Israel in the midst of that pagan society is unfortunate.

So much for their subterfuge. What about their nonkosher lifestyle? Even though the Law of Moses was temporary, and it would be ended with the death of Christ on the cross, that law was still in effect; and the Jews were expected to obey it. Daniel and his friends were careful to obey the law while they lived in Babylon, and the Lord blessed them for their faithfulness (Dan. 1). Why would He overlook the unfaithfulness of Mordecai and Esther *and still use them to accomplish His purposes?*

But even more serious than their lifestyle is the problem of a Jewess in a harem and ultimately marrying a Gentile. The Law of Moses prohibited all kinds of illicit sex as well as mixed marriages (Ex. 20:14; 34:16; Lev. 18; Deut. 7:1-4), and both Ezra and Nehemiah had to deal with the problem of Jews marrying Gentiles (Ezra 9–10; Neh. 10:30; 13:23-27). Yet, God allowed a pure Jewish girl to become the wife of a lustful Gentile pagan king, a worshiper of Zoroaster!

Some Bible students see this whole enterprise as an empire-wide "beauty contest" and Esther as a contestant who probably shouldn't have entered. They also assert that Mordecai encouraged her because he wanted to have a Jew in a place of influence in the empire in case there was trouble. Perhaps that interpretation is true. However, other students feel that the women were not volunteers but were selected and assembled by the king's special officers. The girls were not kidnapped, but everybody knew that the will of an Eastern monarch could not successfully be opposed. In this case I don't think we should condemn Esther for what happened to her since these circumstances were, for the most part, out of her control; and God did overrule them for the good of her people.

When you consider the backslidden state of the Jewish nation at that time, the disobedience of the Jewish remnant in the Persian Empire, and the unspiritual lifestyle of Mordecai and Esther, is it any wonder that the name of God is absent from this book? Would you want to identify your holy name with such an unholy people?

The encouragement of Hegai (Es. 2:8-9). Just as Joseph found favor in Egypt (Gen. 39:21) and Daniel in Babylon (Dan. 1:9), so Esther found favor in Shushan. God is so great that He can work even in the heart and mind of the keeper of a harem! Hegai was a Gentile. His job was to provide pleasure for the king, and he didn't know the true God of Israel. Nevertheless, he played an important role in the plan that God was working out for His people. Even today, God is working in places where you and I might think He is absent.

Hegai had a year-long "beauty treatment" to prepare each woman for the king. It included a prescribed diet, the application of special perfumes and cosmetics, and probably a course on court etiquette. They were being trained to do one thing—satisfy the desires of the king. The one who pleased him the most would become his wife. Because of the providence of God, Hegai gave Esther "special treatment" and the best place in the house for her and her maids.

The nationality of Esther (Es. 2:10-11). Had Esther not been born into the Jewish race, she could never have saved the nation from slaughter. It would appear that the two cousins' silence about their nationality was directed by God because He had a special work for them to accomplish. There was plenty of anti-Semitism in the Gentile world, and Mordecai's motive was probably their own personal safety, but God had something greater in mind. Mordecai and Esther wanted to live in peace, but God used them to keep the Jewish people alive.

The approval of the king (Es. 2:12-18). Each night, a new maiden was brought to the king; and in the morning, she was sent to the house of the concubines, never again to be with the king unless he remembered her and called for her. Such unbridled sensuality eventually would have so bored Ahasuerus that he was probably unable to distinguish one maiden from another. This was not love. It was faceless anonymous lust that craved more and more; and the more the king indulged, the less he was satisfied.

Esther had won the favor of everybody who saw her; and when the king saw her, he responded to her with greater enthusiasm than he had to any of the other women. At last he had found someone to replace Vashti! The phrase "the king loved Esther" (KJV) must not be interpreted to mean that Ahasuerus had suddenly fallen in love with Esther with pure and devoted affection. The NIV rendering is best: "Now the king was attracted to Esther more than to any of the other women" (v. 17). This response was from the Lord who wanted Esther in the royal palace where she could intercede for her people. "Known to God from eternity are all His works" (Acts 15:18, NKJV).

It's worth noting that Esther put herself into the hands of Hegai and did what she was told to do. Hegai knew what the king liked, and, being partial to Esther, he attired her accordingly. Because she possessed such great beauty "in form and features" (Es. 2:7, NIV), Esther didn't require the "extras" that the other women needed. (See 1 Peter 3:1-6.)

The king personally crowned Esther and named her the new queen of the empire. Then he summoned his officials and hosted a great banquet. (This is the fourth banquet in the book. The Persian kings used every opportunity to celebrate!) But the king's generosity even touched the common people, for he proclaimed a national holiday throughout his realm and distributed gifts to the people. This holiday may have been similar to the Hebrew "Year of Jubilee." It's likely that taxes were canceled, servants set free, and workers given a vacation from their jobs. Ahasuerus wanted everybody to feel good about his new queen.

3. The intervention of Mordecai (Es. 2:19-23)

The second "gathering of the virgins" mentioned in verse 19 probably means that the king's officers continued to gather beautiful girls for his harem, for Ahasuerus wasn't likely to become a monogamist and spend the rest of his life with Esther alone. Those who hold that this entire occasion was a "beauty contest" see this second gathering as a farewell to the "candidates" who never got to see the king. They were thanked and sent home. I prefer the first interpretation. Queen or no queen, a man like Ahasuerus wasn't about to release a group of beautiful virgins from his palace!

But most importantly, in verse 19 we now see Mordecai in a position of honor and authority, sitting at the king's gate (4:2; 5:13). In the East, the gate was the ancient equivalent of our modern law courts, the place where important official business was transacted (Ruth 4:1; Dan. 2:48-49). It's possible that Queen Esther used her influence to get her cousin this job.

Once again, we marvel at the providence of God in the life of a man who was not honoring the God of Israel. Neither Mordecai nor Esther had revealed their true nationality. Perhaps we should classify them with Nicodemus and Joseph of Arimathea who were "secret disciples" and yet were used of God to protect and bury the body of Jesus (John 19:38-42).

Like these two men, Mordecai and Esther were "hidden" in the Persian capital because God had a very special work for them to do. Mordecai was able to use his position for the good of both the king and the Jews.

In Eastern courts, palace intrigue was a normal thing. Only a few officers had free access to the king (Es. 1:10, 14), and they often used their privileges to get bribes from people who needed the king's help. (This is why Daniel's fellow officers didn't like him; he was too honest. See Dan. 6.)

It's possible that this assassination attempt was connected with the crowning of the new queen and that Vashti's supporters in the palace resented what Ahasuerus had done. Or perhaps these two men hated Esther because she was an outsider. Although it wasn't consistently obeyed, tradition said that Persian kings should select their wives from women within the seven noble families of the land. These conspirators may have been traditionalists who didn't want a "commoner" on the throne.

Ahasuerus enjoyed almost unlimited authority, wealth, and pleasure. He was insulated from the everyday problems of life (Es. 4:1-4); but this didn't guarantee his personal safety. It was still possible for people to plot against the king and threaten his life. In fact, fourteen years later, Ahasuerus was assassinated!

God in His providence enabled Mordecai to hear about the plot and notify Queen Esther. When Esther told the king, she gave Mordecai the credit for uncovering the conspiracy; and this meant that his name was written into the official chronicle. This fact will play an important part in the drama four years later (6:1ff).

The phrase "hanged on a tree" (Es. 2:23, KJV) probably means "impaled on a stake," one of the usual forms of capital punishment used by the Persians, who were not known for their leniency to prisoners. The usual form of capital punishment among the Jews was stoning; but if they really wanted to humiliate the victim, they would hang the corpse on a tree until sundown (Deut. 21:22-23).

Mordecai received neither recognition nor reward for saving the king's life. No matter; God saw to it that the facts were permanently recorded, and He would make good use of them at the right time. Our good works are like seeds that are planted by faith, and their fruits don't always appear immediately. "Evil pursues sinners, but to the righteous, good shall be repaid" (Prov. 13:21, NKJV). Joseph befriended a fellow prisoner, and the man completely forgot his kindness for two years (Gen. 40:23; 41:1). But God's timing is always perfect, and He sees to it that no good deed is ever wasted.

The plot that Mordecai successfully exposed, however, was nothing compared to the plot he would uncover four years later, planned and perpetrated by Haman, the enemy of the Jews.

An Old Enemy with a New Name

(In which an evil man
challenges the throne of Almighty God)

For four years, things have been peaceful in Shushan. Esther has reigned as queen, and Mordecai has tended to the king's business at the gate. Then everything changed, and all the Jews in the empire found themselves in danger of being killed—just to satisfy the hatred of a man named Haman.

The Book of Esther is one of five Old Testament books that the Jews call "The Writings" or "The Five Megilloth." (The word *megilloth* means "scrolls" in Hebrew.) The other books are Ruth, Ecclesiastes, The Song of Solomon, and Lamentations. Each year on the Feast of Purim, the Book of Esther is read publicly in the synagogue; and whenever the reader mentions Haman's name, the people stamp their feet and exclaim, "May his name be blotted out!" To Jews everywhere, Haman personifies everybody who has tried to exterminate the people of Israel. This chapter explains to us why Haman was such a dangerous man.

1. His ancestry (Es. 3:1a)
Haman was an "Agagite," which could mean he came from a district in the empire known as Agag. But it could also mean

that he was descended from Agag, king of the Amalekites (1 Sam. 15:8). If the latter is the case, then we can easily understand why Haman hated the Jews: God had declared war on the Amalekites and wanted their name and memory blotted off the face of the earth.

The story goes back to the time of Israel's Exodus from Egypt (Ex. 17:8-15), when the Amalekites attacked God's weary people in the rear ranks of the marching nation (Deut. 25:18). After Moses commanded Joshua to fight against Amalek, he interceded on the mountain, and Joshua won a great victory. God told Moses to write in a book that He had declared war on the Amalekites and would one day utterly destroy them because of what they had done to His people. Moses reminded the Israelites of the Amalekites' treacherous attack before they entered the Promised Land (Deut. 25:17-19).

It was Saul, the first king of Israel, whom God commanded to destroy the Amalekites (1 Sam. 15); and he failed in his commission and lost his own crown. (It was an Amalekite who claimed he put Saul to death on the battlefield. See 2 Sam. 1:1-10.) Because Saul didn't fully obey the Lord, some Amalekites lived; and one of their descendants, Haman, determined to annihilate his people's ancient enemy, the Jews. It's worth noting that King Saul, a Benjamite, failed to destroy the Amalekites; but Mordecai, also a Benjamite (Es. 2:5), took up the battle and defeated Haman. It's also worth noting that the founder of the Amalekites was a descendant of Esau (Gen. 36:12), and Esau was the enemy of his brother Jacob. This was another stage in the age-old conflict beween the flesh and the Spirit, Satan and the Lord, the way of faith and the way of the world.

Everything about Haman is hateful; you can't find one thing about this man worth praising. In fact, everything about Haman, *God hated!* "These six things the Lord hates, yes, seven are an abomination to Him: A proud look, a lying tongue, hands that shed innocent blood, a heart that devises wicked plans, feet that are swift in running to evil, a false witness who speaks lies, and one who sows discord among brethren" (Prov. 6:16-19, NKJV). Keep these seven evil characteristics in mind as you read the Book of Esther, for you will see them depicted in this depraved man.

2. His authority (Es. 3:1b)

At some time between the seventh and twelfth years of the reign of Ahasuerus (v. 7; 2:16), the king decided to make Haman chief officer in the empire. Think of it: Mordecai had saved the king's life and didn't receive a word of thanks, let alone a reward; but wicked Haman did nothing and was promoted! There are many seeming injustices in this life; yet God knows what He's doing and will never forsake the righteous or leave their deeds unrewarded. (See Ps. 37.)

Haman probably fawned and flattered his way into this powerful new position because that's the kind of man he was. He was a proud man, and his purpose was to achieve authority and recognition. As we have seen, Ahasuerus was a weak and gullible man, susceptible to flattery and anxious to please people; so Haman's task wasn't a difficult one.

Some Bible students have seen in Haman an illustration of the "man of sin" who will one day appear and ruthlessly rule over humanity (2 Thes. 2; Rev. 13). Haman was given great authority from the king, and Satan will give great power to this wicked world ruler we call the Antichrist (Rev. 13:2, 4). As Haman hated the Jews and tried to destroy them, so the Antichrist will usher in a wave of worldwide anti-Semitism (12:13-17). At first, he will pretend to be friendly to Israel and will even make a covenant to protect them, but then he will break the covenant and oppose the very people he agreed to help (Dan. 9:24-27). As Haman was ultimately defeated and judged, so the Antichrist will be conquered by Jesus Christ and confined to the lake of fire (Rev. 19:11-20).

God permitted Haman to be appointed to this high office because He had purposes to fulfill through him. (See Rom. 9:17.) God takes His promises seriously and will not break His covenant with His people. My friend J. Vernon McGee used to say, "The Jew has attended the funeral of every one of the nations that tried to exterminate him"; and Haman was not to be an exception.

What people do with authority is a test of character. Do they use their authority to promote themselves or to help others? Do they glorify themselves or glorify God? Daniel was given a high position similar to Haman's, but he used his authority to honor God and help others (Dan. 6). Of course, the difference between Daniel and Haman is that Daniel was a humble man of God while Haman was a proud man of the world.

3. His vanity (Es. 3:2-6)
Not content with merely having a high office and using it, Haman wanted all the public recognition and honor that he could secure. Although the ancient people of the Near East were accustomed to giving public displays of homage, the king had to issue a special edict concerning Haman, or the people would not have bowed down to him. Haman was a small man in a big office; and the other nobles, more worthy than he, would not willingly recognize him. This fact is another hint that Haman got the office not by earning it but by stealing it. If he were a worthy officer, the other leaders would have gladly recognized him.

Pride blinds people to what they really are and makes them insist on having what they really don't deserve. The British essayist Walter Savage Landor (1775–1864) wrote, "When little men cast long shadows, it is a sign that the sun is setting." Haman was a little man, indeed, but his vanity compelled him to make himself look and sound bigger than he really was.

"Fools take to themselves the respect that is given to their office," wrote Aesop in his fable "The Jackass in Office"; and it applies perfectly to Haman. He was recognized, not because of his character or his ability, but because of the office he filled and because of the edict of the king. "Try not to become a man of success," said Albert Einstein, "but try to become a man of value." Men and women of value earn the recognition they deserve.

Haman's promotion may have brought out the worst in Haman, but it brought out the best in Mordecai; for Mordecai refused to pay homage to Haman. It must be remembered, however, that the Jews didn't violate the Second Commandment (Ex. 20:4-6) when they bowed down before people in authority any more than Christians do today when they show respect to leaders. For instance, Abraham bowed down to the sons of Heth when he negotiated with them for Sarah's grave (Gen. 23:7). Also Joseph's brothers bowed down before Joseph, thinking he was an Egyptian official (42:6). David even bowed down to Saul (1 Sam. 24:8), and Jacob and his family bowed before Esau (Gen. 33:3, 6-7). The Jews even bowed to one another. (See 2 Sam. 14:4 and 18:28.)

There were crowds of people at the gate, and some of them would be pleading for Haman to intercede for them. Consequently, Haman didn't notice that Mordecai was standing up while everybody else was bowing down. The other officials at the gate questioned Mordecai about his behavior, and it was then that Mordecai openly announced that he was a Jew (Es. 3:3-4). For several days, the royal officials discussed the matter with Mordecai, probably trying to change his mind; and then they reported his behavior to Haman. From that time on, Haman watched Mordecai and nursed his anger, not only toward the man at the gate, but also toward all the Jews in the empire.

Why did Mordecai refuse to bow down to Haman? What was there about being a Jew that prohibited him from doing what everybody else was doing? Even if Mordecai couldn't respect the man, he could at least respect the office and therefore the king who gave Haman the office.

I think the answer is that Haman was an Amalekite, and the Amalekites were the avowed enemies of the Jews. The Lord swore and put in writing that He had declared war on the Amalekites and would fight them from generation to generation (Ex. 17:16). How could Mordecai show homage to the enemy of the Jews and the enemy of the Lord? He didn't want to be guilty of what Joab said about King David, "You love your enemies and hate your friends" (2 Sam. 19:6, NKJV).

Mordecai's controversy with Haman was not a personal quarrel with a proud and difficult man. It was Mordecai's declaration that he was on God's side in the *national* struggle between the Jews and the Amalekites. Mordecai didn't want to make the same mistake his ancestor King Saul had made in being too lenient with God's enemies (1 Sam. 15). Because Saul compromised with the Amalekites, he lost his crown; but because Mordecai opposed them, he eventually gained a crown (Es. 8:15).

Keep in mind that the extermination of the Jews would mean the end of the messianic promise for the world. The reason God promised to protect His people was that they might become the channel through whom He might give the Word of God and the Son of God to the world. Israel was to bring the blessing of salvation to all nations (Gen. 12:1-3; Gal. 3:7-18). Mordecai wasn't nurturing a personal grudge against Haman so much as enlisting in the perpetual battle God has with those who work for the devil and try to hinder His will in this world (Gen. 3:15).

Mordecai is not the only person in the Bible who for conscience' sake practiced "civil disobedience." The Hebrew midwives disobeyed Pharaoh's orders and refused to kill the Jewish babies (Ex. 1:15-22). Daniel and his three friends refused to eat the king's food (Dan. 1), and the three friends also refused to bow down to Nebuchadnezzar's image (Dan. 3). The apostles refused to stop witnessing in Jerusalem and affirmed, "We must obey God rather than men" (Acts 5:29). That statement can be a wonderful declaration of faith or a cowardly evasion of responsibility, depending on the heart of the person saying it.

But please note that, in each of these instances, *the people had a direct word from God that gave them assurance they were doing His will.* And further note that, in every instance, the believers were kind and respectful. They didn't start riots or burn down buildings "for conscience' sake." Because civil authority is ordained of God (Rom. 13), it's a serious thing for Christians to disobey the law; and if we're going to do it, we must know the difference between personal prejudices and biblical convictions.

Something else is involved: By confessing that he was a Jew, Mordecai was asking for trouble for both himself and the other Jews in the empire. *Obedience to conscience and the will of God in defiance of civil law is not a casual thing to be taken lightly.* Some of the "conscience protesters" we've seen on television, however, have seemed more like clowns going to a party than soldiers going to a battle. They could never stand with people like Martin Luther who challenged prelates and potentates with: "My conscience is captive to the Word of God. Here I stand, I cannot do otherwise!"

Mordecai may have had shortcomings with reference to his religious practices, but we must admire him for his courageous stand. Certainly God had put him and Esther into their official positions so that they might save their people from annihilation. Their neglect of the Jewish law is incidental when you consider their courage in risking their lives.

Like a cancerous tumor, Haman's hatred for Mordecai soon developed into hatred for the whole Jewish race. Haman could have reported Mordecai's crime to the king, and the king would have imprisoned Mordecai or perhaps had him executed; but that would not have satisfied Haman's lust for revenge. No, his hatred had to be nourished by something bigger, like the destruction of a whole nation. As with Judas in the Upper Room, so with Haman in the palace: he became a murderer. Mark Twain called anti-Semitism "the swollen envy of pygmy minds." And he was right.

4. His subtlety (Es. 3:7-15a)

Follow the steps that wicked Haman took as he executed his plan to destroy the Jewish people.

He selected the day (Es. 3:7). Haman and some of the court astrologers cast lots to determine the day for the Jews' destruction. This was done privately before Haman approached the king with his plan. Haman wanted to be sure that his gods were with him and that his plan would succeed.

The Eastern peoples in that day took few important steps without consulting the stars and the omens. A century before, when King Nebuchadnezzar and his generals couldn't agree on a campaign strategy, they paused to consult their gods. "For the king of Babylon stands at the parting of the road, at the fork of the two roads, to use divination: he shakes the arrows, he consults the images, he looks at the liver" (Ezek. 21:21, NKJV).[1] The Babylonian word *puru* means

---

[1] "Shaking the arrows" was something like our modern "drawing straws," with the arrows marked with the possible choices of action. "Consulting images" had to do with seeking help from the images of the gods they carried with them. "Looking at the liver" involved offering an animal sacrifice and getting directions from the shape and marks on the liver.

"lot," and from it the Jews get the name of their feast, Purim (Es. 9:26).

It's interesting that Haman began this procedure in the month of Nisan, the very month in which the Jews celebrated their deliverance from Egypt. As the astrologers cast lots over the calendar, month by month and day by day, they arrived at the most propitious date: the thirteenth day of the twelfth month (v. 13). This decision was certainly of the Lord, because it gave the Jews a whole year to get ready, and because it would also give Mordecai and Esther time to act. "The lot is cast into the lap; but the whole disposing thereof is of the Lord" (Prov. 16:33, KJV).

Was Haman disappointed with this choice? He may have wanted to act immediately, catch the Jews off guard, and satisfy his hatred much sooner. On the other hand, he would have nearly a year in which to nurse his grudge and anticipate revenge, and that would be enjoyable. He could watch the Jews panic, knowing that he was in control. Even if the Jews took advantage of this delay and moved out of the empire, he would still get rid of them and be able to claim whatever goods and property they would have left behind. The plan seemed a good one.

He requested the king's permission (Es. 3:8-11). Like Satan, the great enemy of the Jews, Haman was both a murderer and a liar (John 8:44). To begin with, he didn't even give the king the name of the people who were supposed to be subverting the kingdom. His vague description of the situation made the danger seem even worse. The fact that these dangerous people were scattered throughout the whole empire made it even more necessary that the king do something about them.

Haman was correct when he described the Jews as a people whose "laws are different from those of all other people" (Es. 3:8). Their laws were different because they were God's chosen people who alone received God's holy law from His own hand. Moses asked, "And what great nation is there that has such statutes and righteous judgments as are in all this law which I set before you this day?" (Deut. 4:8, NKJV) and the answer is: "None!"

The fact that one man, Mordecai, disobeyed one law was exaggerated by Haman into the false accusation that *all* the Jews disobeyed *all* the laws of the land. The Prophet Jeremiah had instructed the Jews of the Exile to behave as good citizens and cooperate with their captors (Jer. 29:4-7), and the evidence seems to be that they obeyed. If the Jews in the Persian Empire had been repeatedly guilty of sedition or treason, Ahasuerus would have known about it by now. And even if some Jews in a few towns did disobey the king's laws, why should the whole nation of Israel be destroyed for the crimes of a few?

Haman's *coup de grace* came at the end of his speech when he offered to pay the king 10,000 talents of silver for the privilege of ridding the empire of these dangerous people. According to the Greek historian Herodotus (Book III, Section 95), the annual income of the entire Persian Empire was 15,000 talents of silver. In effect, Haman was offering the king an amount equivalent to two thirds of that huge amount. Haman must have been a fabulously wealthy man. Of course, he hoped to recoup some of this amount from the spoils taken from the Jews.

In Esther 3:11, the king's response ("The silver is given to thee," KJV) gives the impression that Ahasuerus rejected the money and offered to pay the expenses himself. In typical Oriental fashion, the king politely rejected the offer ("Keep the money," NIV), fully expecting Haman to insist that he accept it. (See Abraham's bargaining with the sons of Heth, Gen. 23.) Haman knew that the Greek wars had impoverished the king's treasuries, and he would never have offered so much money to so mighty a ruler if he didn't really intend to pay it. (See Es. 4:7.)

Without asking any questions, the king gave Haman his royal signet ring (see 8:2, 8), which granted him the authority to act in the king's name. He could write any document he pleased and put the king's seal on it, and the document had to be accepted as law and obeyed. It was a foolish thing for Ahasuerus to do; but true to character, he acted first and regretted it afterward. "He who answers a matter before he hears it, it is folly and shame to him" (Prov. 18:13, NKJV).

He immediately spread the word (Es. 3:12-14). Unknown to the Jews who were getting ready to celebrate Passover, Haman was busy with the king's secretaries, writing out the new law and translating it into the various languages of the peoples within the empire. In verse 13, the words of the law are similar to the instructions Samuel gave to King Saul when he sent him to destroy the Amalekites (1 Sam. 15:1-3). The one important difference was that Saul was not permitted to take any of the spoil, while Haman and his helpers hoped to plunder the Jews and accumulate great wealth. The official document was given to the royal couriers, who quickly carried it to every part of the empire.

If, in an ancient kingdom, a message of bad news could be so quickly prepared, translated, and distributed, why does it take the church so long to disseminate the good news of salvation through faith in Jesus Christ? To be sure, we have more people in our modern world than Ahasuerus had in his empire, but we also have better means of communication and transportation. *The problem must be with the couriers.* The message is ready to go, but we don't have enough people to carry it and enough money to send them.

The work was done quickly because Haman didn't want Ahasuerus to change his mind. Once the law was written and sealed, the doom of the Jews was also sealed; for the laws of the Medes and Persians could not be altered (Es. 1:19; 8:8; Dan. 6:8). Haman's subtle plan had worked.

5. His apathy (Es. 3:15b)

Haman could send out the death warrants for thousands of innocent people and then sit down to a banquet with the king! What a calloused heart he had! He was like the people the Prophet Amos described: "that drink wine in bowls, and anoint themselves with the chief ointments; but they are not grieved for the affliction of Joseph" (Amos 6:6). However, in the end, it was his own death warrant that Haman had sealed; for within less than three months, Haman would be a dead man (Es. 8:9).

Helen Keller said, "Science may have found a cure for most evils, but it has found no remedy for the worst of them all—the apathy of human beings" *(My Religion,* p. 162). Jesus vividly illustrated that apathy in the Parable of the Good Samaritan (Luke 10:25-37). He pointed out that two religious men, a priest and a Levite, ignored the needs of the dying man, while the Samaritan, a hated outsider, sacrificed to take care of him. Jesus also made it clear that loving the Lord ought to make us love our neighbor, and our neighbor is anyone who needs us.

Therefore, before we condemn wicked Haman, let's examine our own hearts. Billions of lost sinners in today's world are under a sentence of *eternal* death, and most Christians do very little about it. We can sit at our church banquets and Sunday dinners without even thinking about helping to get the message out that "the Father has sent the Son to be the Savior of the world" (1 John 4:14).

In June 1865, missionary to China, J. Hudson Taylor, had gone to stay with friends at Brighton, a popular British resort city by the sea. He was weary and ill and seeking the will of God for the future of his ministry. On Sunday, June 25, "unable to bear the sight of rejoicing multitudes in the house of God," he went for a walk on the sands and wrestled with God in agony of soul. God met him in a fresh way, and he trusted God to provide twenty-four workers to labor with him in China. Two days later, he went to the London & County Bank and opened an account in the name of the China Inland Mission! It was the beginning of a miracle ministry that continues today.[2]

The phrase in the account that tugs at my heart is "unable to bear the sight of rejoicing multitudes in the house of God." Certainly it's good to rejoice in the Lord and to do it in His house, but rejoicing must never be a substitute for responsibility. As a popular Gospel song expresses it: "God's tables are full but His fields are empty." We all want to enjoy the feast, but we don't want to share the message. We don't have to be hardened unbelievers like Haman to be apathetic and unconcerned about the plight of the world's billions of lost souls.

In contrast to the happiness of the king and his prime minister were the heaviness and bewilderment of the people in Shusan, Gentiles and Jews alike. What had caused this sudden change in policy? Why were the Jews suddenly targeted as enemies of the empire? Was there any way of escape?

The situation was not hopeless, however, for God had two people prepared and in place — Mordecai and Queen Esther — and He was ready to act.

---

[2]See *Hudson Taylor and the China Inland Mission: The Growth of a Work of God,* pp. 31–32.

A Day of Decision

(In which the queen goes into her
counting house and counts the cost)

There were perhaps 15 million Jews scattered throughout the Persian Empire. Because of Haman's enmity and the king's stupidity, all of them were now appointed to die, unless they pulled up stakes and left the kingdom. But if they did that, where would they go? Even their own land of Israel wasn't safe because it was under the rule of Ahasuerus. Since the Persians ruled "from India to Ethiopia" (1:1), there were very few accessible places to which the Jews might flee.

In the empire, the responses to Haman's decree were varied. Haman and the king completely ignored the plight of the Jews and sat down to a royal feast. Meanwhile, the people of the capital city were perplexed and didn't know what to do (3:15). Secluded in the royal harem, Queen Esther knew nothing about the danger that she and her people faced. While the Jews in the various provinces began to fast and mourn (4:3), only one man, Mordecai, was able to do anything about the peril; and he immediately began to act.

1. He expressed his concern (Es. 4:1-3)

Mordecai's appearance and actions (v. 1) were those of a person showing great grief (2 Sam. 1:11-12; 13:19) or deep repentance (Jonah 3; Neh. 9:1-2). Mordecai was neither afraid nor ashamed to let people know where he stood. He had already told the officers at the gate that he was a Jew; now he was telling the whole city that he was not only a Jew but also that he opposed the murderous edict. Although it can't be documented from his writings, a statement usually attributed to the British politician Edmund Burke certainly applies here: "All that is required for evil to triumph is for good men to do nothing."

"Deliver those who are drawn toward death, and hold back those stumbling to the slaughter. If you say, 'Surely we did not know this,' does not He who weighs the hearts consider it? He who keeps your soul, does He not know it? And will He not render to each man according to his deeds?" These solemn words from Proverbs 24:11-12 (NKJV) make it clear that we can't be neutral when human lives are at stake.

Mordecai ended his mournful pilgrimage at the king's gate, which was the commercial and legal hub of the city, a combination of marketplace and courtroom. That was as far as he could go because Oriental kings lived in an artificial paradise that sheltered them from the realities of life. "No sackcloth must come within their gates," said Scottish preacher George H. Morrison. "They must have a good time at any cost. They must live their easy and comfortable lives, as if there were no voices calling them" *(The Afterglow of God,* p. 72). How opposite from our Priest-King in heaven who welcomes us to bring our burdens and sorrows to Him!

What could Mordecai hope to accomplish at the gate with his sackcloth and his wailing? Well, perhaps somebody from the palace would take notice of him and get a message to Queen Esther. The queen's ladies-in-waiting knew Mordecai (Es. 2:11), although they didn't know the relationship between him and the queen; and Mordecai had already transmitted information to the queen through some of her retainers (2:22). Since Mordecai couldn't enter the house of the women, this was his only hope.

Esther received the report that Mordecai was dressed in sackcloth and ashes, mourning at the king's gate. Since she wasn't told the reason for her cousin's strange conduct, she did the logical thing and sent him fine clothes to put on lest his sackcloth arouse the concern of the king's officers and guards. What if the king should come out to the gate for an audience with the people? Mordecai would then be in trouble.

The queen's motives were fine, but her method was faulty. Before sending the new clothes to Mordecai, she should have found out what the problem really was. If Ahasuerus did appear at the gate, Mordecai's courtly garments might save him temporarily from the wrath of the king; but they couldn't rescue the Jews from the penalty of death that Haman had issued for them. Mordecai's mourning, however, finally got the attention of the queen; and that's what he wanted.

2. He explained their peril (Es. 4:4-9)
Mordecai's refusal of the new clothes gave him opportunity to get his vital message to the queen, for she sent one of her eunuchs to the gate to ask Mordecai what was wrong. I doubt that Hathach realized what an important part he was playing in God's plan to defeat Haman and save the Jews. So often in the work of the Lord, He uses obscure people to accomplish important tasks. What was the name of the lad who gave Jesus his loaves and fishes? Who were the men who rescued Paul by lifting him over that Damascus wall in a basket? What was the name of the little servant girl who told Naaman to go see the prophet? We don't know, but God used these people to accomplish His purposes. As great doors can swing upon small hinges, so great events can turn upon the deeds of "small" and sometimes anonymous people.

Mordecai not only knew all the facts about the decree, but

he also had a copy of it for Esther to read for herself. This proves that he held a high position in the government, a position God had given him for the very purpose of saving the Jewish nation. But Mordecai did much more than inform the queen. He urged her to reveal her true nationality and go to the royal throne and intercede for her people.

When Mordecai told Hathach to tell the queen to ask for mercy "for her people," he divulged to him the fact that Esther was a Jewess. Did it shock Hathach, or was he perhaps a Jew himself, and that's why Mordecai entrusted him with this secret? Like Daniel and his three friends in Babylon, Jewish exiles in the Persian Empire were often pressed into royal service.

Now, the big question was: how would Queen Esther respond to this crisis?

3. He exhorted the queen (Es. 4:10-14)
Keep in mind that Mordecai couldn't speak directly to Esther but had to send his messages to her via Hathach. Esther had no way of sensing *personally* how Mordecai felt, nor could Mordecai fully understand how Esther was expressing herself. What a difference it makes when we can see the faces and hear the voices of the people we communicate with! Hathach certainly had a great responsibility placed on him as the living link between two distressed people who held in their hands the salvation of the Jewish nation.

In verses 10-11, Esther's reply was not an evasion but an explanation. She reminded Mordecai of what he already knew, that nobody, not even the queen, could rush into the throne room and ask for an immediate audience with the king. If she were to do so, she would take her life in her hands. Not only was the king of Persia sheltered from seeing sorrow and hearing bad news, but he was also protected from interruptions that might interfere with his schedule.

Again, I don't think this was an excuse on Esther's part, but rather a plea that Mordecai give her some guidance. He knew palace protocol, he was a man, and he was in touch with what was going on. She was isolated in the harem and incapable of devising the kind of strategy needed to solve the problem. Besides all this, she hadn't seen the king for a month; and it was possible that she had somehow fallen out of favor. Ahasuerus was unpredictable, and Esther didn't want to make matters worse.

I get the impression that Mordecai misinterpreted Esther's message. It sounded to him like she was trying to hide her nationality and avoid the responsibility of presenting herself to the king. Had he seen and heard her in person, he probably would have judged her differently.

In his reply, Mordecai reminded Esther of three solemn facts. First, he told her that her being a palace resident was no guarantee that she would be delivered from death. The royal edict said "all the Jews" (3:13), and Haman would see to it that every last Jew was discovered and slain, even those in the palace. For that matter, there were probably palace personnel who were still loyal to Vashti and would be happy to see Queen Esther removed.

Second, Mordecai reminded her that her silence wouldn't prevent deliverance from coming from some other source. The reference here is to the providence of God even though the name of God isn't mentioned. Knowing the Abrahamic Covenant (Gen. 12:1-3), Mordecai had faith that the people of Israel would be protected from annihilation. However, he warned her that even if deliverance did come, some of the Jews might still be slain, and Esther might be among them.

Why would God send "relief and deliverance" (NIV) to the Jewish people but allow Esther and her relatives to be slain? Perhaps Mordecai saw this as a punishment for her unwillingness to intercede for the people. To know to do good and not do it is sin (James 4:17). Therefore, instead of protecting herself by her silence, Esther would be putting herself into greater jeopardy. Haman and his agents would have little trouble finding her in the palace and taking her life.

Mordecai emphasized a third fact: Her being in the palace was not an accident, for she had "come to royal position for such a time as this" (Es. 4:14, NIV). He didn't say that God had put her there, but that's what his statement amounted to. If Esther would just take the time to review her life, she couldn't help but see that there had been divine leading all the way. Now, if God brought her to the throne, then He had a purpose in mind, and that purpose was now evident: She was there to intercede for her people. The statement of Joseph to his brothers comes to mind: "But as for you, you meant evil against me; but God meant it for good, in order to bring it about as it is this day, to save many people alive" (Gen. 50:20, NKJV).

As you ponder Mordecai's words, you will learn some basic truths about the providence of God that are important for Christians today. The first is that *God has divine purposes to accomplish in this world.* God's purposes involve the Jewish nation as well as the Gentile nations of the world. They also involve the church. God deals with individuals as well as with nations. His purposes touch the lives of kings and queens and common people, godly people and wicked people. There is nothing in this world that is outside the influence of the purposes of God.

Mordecai made it clear that *God accomplishes His purposes through people.* For reasons we don't fully understand, God permits wicked people to do evil things in this world; but He can work in and through unbelievers and His own people to accomplish His purposes. While He was not the author of his sins, God permitted the king's drunkenness and his foolishness in deposing Vashti. He used the king's loneliness to place Esther on the throne; and, in chapter 6, he will use the king's sleeplessness to reward Mordecai and start to overthrow the power of Haman. In great things and little things, God is sovereign.

The third truth that Mordecai emphasized was that *God will accomplish His purposes even if His servants refuse to obey His will.* If Esther rejected the will of God for her life, God could still save His people; but Esther would be the loser. When ministers and missionaries appeal to the church for volunteers for Christian service, they sometimes give the impression that God's work is at the mercy of God's workers; but this isn't true.

If you and I refuse to obey God, He can either *abandon us* and get somebody else to do the job, and we will lose the reward and blessing; or He can *discipline us* until we surrender to His will. Two examples come to mind. Since John Mark left the mission field and returned home (Acts 13:13; 15:36-41), God raised up Timothy to take his place (16:1-3). When Jonah ran from God, the Lord kept after him until he obeyed, even though he didn't obey from his heart. When God isn't permitted to rule, He overrules; and He always accomplishes His purposes.

The fourth lesson from Mordecai's speech is that *God isn't in a hurry but will fulfill His plans in due time.* God waited until the third year of the king's reign before taking Vashti off the throne. Then he waited another four years (Es. 2:16) before putting Esther on the throne. It was not until the king's twelfth year (3:7) that God allowed Haman to hatch his evil plot, and He decreed that the "crisis day" for the Jews would be almost a year away.

If you were reading the Book of Esther for the first time, you might become impatient with God and conclude that He was doing nothing. In chapters 1 and 2, a drunken king and his flattering advisers seem to be in charge. From chapter 3 to chapter 6, it looks as though wicked Haman is in control. Even after Haman is off the scene, it's the king's unalterable decree that keeps everybody busy. *But where is God?*

God is never in a hurry. He knows the end from the beginning, and His decrees are always right and always on time. Dr. A.W. Tozer compared God's sovereign purposes to an ocean liner, leaving New York City, bound for Liverpool, England. The people on board the ship are free to do as they please, but they aren't free to change the course of the ship.

"The mighty liner of God's sovereign design keeps its steady course over the sea of history," wrote Dr. Tozer. "God moves undisturbed and unhindered toward the fulfillment of those eternal purposes which He purposed in Christ Jesus before the world began" *(The Knowledge of the Holy,* p. 118).

The sovereignty of God doesn't suggest fatalism or blind determinism, both of which would make life a prison. Only a sovereign God is great enough to decree freedom of choice for men and women, and only a sovereign God could fulfill His wise and loving purposes in this world and even make evil cooperate in producing good (Gen. 50:20). The question is not, "Is God in control of this world?" but, "Is God in control of my life?" Are we cooperating with Him so that we are a part of the answer and not a part of the problem?

To quote Dr. Tozer again: "In the moral conflict now raging around us whoever is on God's side is on the winning side and cannot lose; whoever is on the other side is on the losing side and cannot win" (p. 119).

4. He expedited the plan (Es. 4:15-17)

When we first met Esther and Mordecai, they were hiding their identity as Jews. Now Mordecai is enlisting other Jews in the struggle against Haman, and Esther is commanding her Gentile ladies-in-waiting to participate in the fast!

Even though the name of God is not mentioned in the text, this act of humiliation was obviously directed to the Lord and was certainly accompanied by prayer. Fasting and prayer are frequently found together in Scripture, for fasting is a preparation for concentrated and humble prayer. (See Ezra 8:21-23; Ps. 35:13; Dan. 9:3; Acts 13:3.) Of itself, fasting is no guarantee that God will bless, for fasting must be accompanied by sincere humility and brokenness before the Lord (Isa. 58:1-10; Joel 2:12-13; Matt. 6:16-18). If fasting is only a formal religious ritual, it accomplishes no spiritual purpose.

Since Jews throughout the empire were already "fasting, weeping, and wailing" (Es. 4:3), it wasn't difficult for Mordecai to unite the Jews in Shushan to pray for Esther as she prepared to intercede before the king. This was a matter of life and death both for her and her people, and God used the crisis that Haman had created to bring a spiritual revival to His people scattered among the Gentiles. It's often the case that God's people have to experience trouble before they will humble themselves and cry out to God.

How should we interpret Esther's words, "And if I perish, I perish"? Do these words suggest unbelieving resignation ("Well, you forced me into it, so I'll do what you say, even if it kills me!") or trustful submission to the will of God ("I'll do God's will, whatever the cost!")? I vote for the second interpretation. To me, Esther echoes the same surrender and confidence that Paul expressed to the Ephesian elders: "But none of these things move me, neither count I my life dear unto myself, so that I might finish my course with joy, and the ministry, which I have received of the Lord Jesus, to testify the gospel of the grace of God" (Acts 20:24, KJV).

From the human point of view, everything was against Esther and the success of her mission. The law was against her, because nobody was allowed to interrupt the king. The government was against her, for the decree said that she was

115

to be slain. Her sex was against her, because the king's attitude toward women was worse than chauvinistic. The officers were against her, because they did only those things that ingratiated themselves with Haman. In one sense, even the fast could be against her; for going three days without food and drink would not necessarily improve her appearance or physical strength. But "if God be for us, who can be against us?" (Rom. 8:31, KJV)

The answer of faith is — "Nobody!"

A Day in the Life of the Prime Minister

(In which an evil man gathers
enough rope to hang himself)

In recent years, the news media have had a heyday reporting the questionable (and usually illegal) behavior of well-known people, including professional athletes, politicians, preachers, presidents of financial institutions, and even royalty. From "Watergate" to "Iran Gate" to "Pearly Gate," the investigative reporters have been kept busy digging up news to satisfy the public's insatiable appetite for scandal.

If all this journalistic activity accomplished nothing else, it certainly underscored the significance of the biblical warning, "Be sure your sin will find you out" (Num. 32:23, NKJV). People may succeed for a time in covering up disgraceful activities, but eventually the truth surfaces, and everybody knows what's going on. And the culprit discovers that *the wrong we do to others, we do to ourselves.*

The words of Psalm 7:14-16 make me think of Haman: "He who is pregnant with evil and conceives trouble gives birth to disillusionment. He who digs a hole and scoops it out falls into the pit he has made. The trouble he causes recoils on himself; his violence comes down on his own head" (NIV).

There is a law of retribution in this world declaring that the person who maliciously seeks to destroy others ends up destroying himself. The French existentialist Albert Camus wrote in his novel *The Fall:* "There's no need to hang about waiting for the last judgment—it takes place every day."

Though the mills of God grind slowly,
yet they grind exceeding small;
Though with patience He stands waiting,
with exactness grinds He all.
(Friedrich von Logau)

Haman didn't realize it, but four forces had already begun to work together to destroy him.

1. Divine sovereignty (Es. 5:1-5)

Esther was concerned whether the king would acknowledge her presence and grant her an audience. If he didn't, it could mean her immediate execution; and she knew how unpredictable were his moods. The Jews had been fasting and praying for three days, asking God to intervene and save them from annihilation; and now Esther had to act.

What Esther did ranks among the great deeds of faith in Scripture and could have been recorded in Hebrews 11. It wasn't enough for the Jews to pray and have faith that God would work. Somebody had to act, for "faith without works is dead" (James 2:20, KJV). But Esther wasn't operating on the basis of "blind faith." She knew that God had covenanted with the Jews to deal with their enemies (Gen. 12:1-3). She also knew that the God of Israel was a forgiving God who would hear His people when they humbled themselves and prayed (2 Chron. 7:14). Furthermore, God had allowed a remnant of Jews to return to their land and rebuild the temple. Surely it wasn't God's will that they perish and their work stop.

Unlike Esther, when we come to the throne of grace, we

don't have to wonder what our Father thinks about us because He always loves His people and welcomes them into His presence. *One of the greatest needs in the church today is for intercessors who will pray faithfully for a lost world and for a church that desperately needs revival.* "And He saw that there was no man, and wondered that there was no intercessor" (Isa. 59:16, KJV). When the needs are so great and the privilege of prayer is so wonderful, well might the Lord wonder that His people neglect the throne of grace. As John Newton wrote:

> Thou art coming to a King,
> Large petitions with thee bring;
> For His grace and power are such
> None can ever ask too much.

Let's note that Esther *prepared herself to meet the king.* (You'll recall that Ruth prepared herself to meet Boaz. See chap. 3.) If you knew you were going to meet the President of the United States at the White House, or royalty at Buckingham Palace, you would prepare for the meeting. Like Peter sinking into the sea, there are times when we have to rush into God's presence and cry out for help. But the power of those "emergency prayers" depends on our day-by-day fellowship with God, and that fellowship demands preparation. Preparing to pray is as important as the praying itself.

The king officially recognized his queen and invited her to share her petition. "There are many devices in a man's heart; nevertheless the counsel of the Lord, that shall stand" (Prov. 19:21, KJV). "The king's heart is in the hand of the Lord, as the rivers of water: He turneth it whithersoever He will" (Prov. 21:1, KJV; see Ezra 6:22). The sovereign God was in control.

Why didn't Esther immediately inform the king about Haman's evil plot? For at least four reasons. For one thing, it wasn't *the right time*. The king was unprepared to receive the shocking news that his number one officer was a scoundrel. In the midst of kingdom business, Ahasuerus might have considered her accusation an act of treason if not just a piece of palace gossip.

But neither was it *the right place* for her to intercede. There were no doubt retainers serving the king in the throne room, and it would have been a breach of palace etiquette for the queen to make her plea publicly. The sight of a weeping, pleading woman before the throne might have annoyed the king and made matters worse. Better she should speak to the king in the privacy of her own apartment than in the throne room.

The third reason was that Esther wanted Haman, *and only Haman*, present when she told the king about his prime minister's evil plot. With womanly intuition, Esther was confident that Haman, caught off-guard, would in some way admit his guilt and do something foolish that would anger the king. It turned out that she was right on both counts.

But there was a fourth reason—one that Esther herself was unaware of at that time. One more event had to intervene before she could share her burden with the king, and it would take place that very night. The king would discover that he had never rewarded Mordecai for saving his life five years before, and he would rectify that mistake immediately. He would honor Mordecai, but at the same time humiliate Haman; and this experience would help prepare the king to hear Esther's petition.

Esther's banquet was already prepared. Thus, Haman and the king had to hurry to attend. In answer to prayer, God so worked in the king's heart that he not only cooperated willingly with his queen but he also made Haman cooperate. Such is the wonder of the providence of God.

2. False confidence (Es. 5:6-9a)

What an honor for Haman to attend a special banquet with the king and queen *alone* and in the queen's private apartment at that! It's unlikely that any official in the empire had ever been so honored. As Haman ate and drank with Ahasuerus and Esther, his confidence grew. He was indeed an important man in the kingdom, and his future was secure.

When the king asked Esther to state her petition, it gave the prime minister even more confidence; for here were the king and queen discussing a personal matter in his presence! Haman was not only the king's confidant, but now he was sharing in the intimate concerns of the queen as well. Since the queen had invited him to the banquet, she must certainly value his counsel.

At the banquet, we see three more evidences of the sovereignty of God. First, the Lord restrained Esther from telling Ahasuerus the truth about Haman. While there may have been fear in her heart, I don't think that's what held her back. The Lord was working in her life and directing what she said, even though she wasn't aware of it. God was delaying the great exposure until after the king had honored Mordecai.

We also see the sovereign hand of God at work in the way the king accepted the delay and agreed to come to the second banquet. Monarchs like Ahasuerus aren't accustomed to being told to wait. "To man belong the plans of the heart, but from the Lord comes the reply of the tongue" (Prov. 16:1, NIV). "Many are the plans in a man's heart, but it is the Lord's purpose that prevails" (19:21, NIV). Whatever plans Ahasuerus had made for the next evening were canceled to make time for the queen's second feast.

A third evidence of God's sovereignty is that none of Esther's attendants who knew that she was a Jewess tried to convey this important information to Haman. Had Haman known the queen's nationality, he would have immediately devised some plan to prevent her from interfering. Palace intrigue is a dangerous game, and any of the attendants could have profited by telling Haman what they knew.

The fact that Esther invited Haman to the second banquet only increased this evil man's confidence (Es. 5:12), and that's exactly the response the queen wanted. As long as her enemy was overconfident, she knew it would lead to a fall. "He who trusts in himself is a fool, but he who walks in wisdom is kept safe" (Prov. 28:26, NIV). Like the rich fool in our Lord's parable (Luke 12:16-21), Haman was confident that he was set for life, when in reality he was just a few hours away from death.

Two other men come to mind whose false confidence led to their death: King Belshazzar and Judas Iscariot. King Belshazzar held a great feast during which he blasphemed the God of Israel; and by sending handwriting on the wall, God announced his doom. That very night Babylon was conquered and Belshazzar was slain (Dan. 5).

Judas, an apostle of the Lord, was not a true believer (John 6:70-71) but a traitor and a thief (12:6). In the Upper Room, he sat in the place of honor at the table, and none of the other disciples knew what was in his heart. But Jesus knew what Judas was and what Judas would do, and He hid this knowledge from the disciples. In fact, Jesus even washed Judas' feet! Confident that he had everything under control, Judas betrayed Jesus to the enemy and ended up committing suicide (Matt. 27:1-10).

The only safe place to put your confidence is in the Lord.

3. Pride (Es. 5:10-12)

The famous actor John Barrymore said, "One of my chief regrets during my years in the theater is that I couldn't sit in the audience and watch me."

It was with that kind of an attitude that Haman left the

palace and returned home with a joyful heart. Fresh from an intimate dinner with the king and queen, and anticipating a second banquet the next evening, Haman launched himself on an ego trip that disgusts me each time I read it. Note the number of masculine personal pronouns here: *his* friends, *his* wife, *his* riches, *his* sons. (He had ten; 9:7-10.) The king had promoted *him* above everybody else. I'm reminded of that rich farmer in Luke 12:16-21 whose favorite word was *I*.

Didn't Haman know that "pride goes before destruction, and a haughty spirit before a fall"? (Prov. 16:18, NKJV) Or that "a man's pride will bring him low"? (29:23, NKJV) Anybody who boasts about position, wealth, family, or anything else ought to heed the words of John the Baptist: "A man can receive nothing, except it be given him from heaven" (John 3:27, KJV). "For who makes you differ from another?" asked Paul. "And what do you have that you did not receive? Now if you did indeed receive it, why do you glory as if you had not received it?" (1 Cor. 4:7, NKJV)

Many theologians are of the conviction that pride is the very essence of sin. (Perhaps that's why pride is number one on God's "hate list." See Prov. 6:16-19.) It was pride that turned Lucifer into Satan: "I will be like the Most High" (Isa. 14:14, NKJV). Satan used pride to tempt Eve: "You will be like God" (Gen. 3:5, NIV). British Bible scholar William Barclay wrote, "Pride is the ground in which all the other sins grow, and the parent from which all the other sins come."

What does a sinful person have to be proud of? We certainly can't be proud of our ancestry. The Puritan preacher William Jenkyn said, "Our father was Adam, our grandfather dust, and our great-grandfather—nothing." So much for the family tree! The only thing the Bible says is great about humanity is its sin: "And God saw that the wickedness of man was great in the earth" (Gen. 6:5, KJV). So much for our achievements!

123

Someone has said that pride is the only known disease that makes everybody sick except the person who has it. Unless cured, pride is a sickness unto death.

4. Malice (Es. 5:9b, 13-14)

When Haman left the queen's palace, he was walking on air; but the sight of Mordecai immediately brought him down to earth again. On previous occasions, Mordecai had refused to bow down to Haman (3:4-5), but now the courageous Jew even refused to stand up and acknowledge the presence of the illustrious prime minister. I once attended a press briefing at the White House; and when President Reagan entered the room, we all stood to our feet. When a presiding judge enters a courtroom, everyone rises and remains standing until the judge is seated. Whether we like the President or the judge personally is not the issue. We all show respect to the offices that they hold.

Haman was "filled with rage against Mordecai" (5:9, NIV). His hatred of the Jews in general and Mordecai in particular had so poisoned his system that he couldn't even enjoy talking about his greatness! "But all this gives me no satisfaction," he admitted, "as long as I see that Jew Mordecai sitting at the king's gate" (v. 13, NIV).

Malice is that deep-seated hatred that brings delight if our enemy suffers and pain if our enemy succeeds. Malice can never forgive; it must always take revenge. Malice has a good memory for hurts and a bad memory for kindnesses. In 1 Corinthians 5:8, Paul compared malice to yeast, because, like yeast, malice begins very small but gradually grows and finally permeates the whole of life. Malice in the Christian's heart grieves the Holy Spirit and must be put out of our lives (Eph. 4:30-32; Col. 3:8).

The insidious thing about malice is that it has to act; eventually it must express itself. But when you shoot at your enemy, beware! For the ammunition usually ricochets off the target and comes back to wound the shooter! If a person wants to self-destruct, the fastest way to do it is to be like Haman and cultivate a malicious spirit.

Haman had infected his wife and friends with his sinful hatred of the Jews, and they suggested that he ask the king for permission to hang Mordecai. A man with Haman's authority could always trump up some charge, and the king wasn't about to take time to investigate. *Of course, this was before Ahasuerus discovered that Mordecai had saved his life!* Now we can better understand Esther's delay in offering her petition to the king. After the events in chapter 6, it would be impossible for Haman to get permission to execute Mordecai.

Not one to waste time, Haman ordered that the gallows be made. We're not sure whether the gallows itself was seventy-five feet high or whether it was put in a prominent place that lifted it to that height, such as the city wall or the roof of a building. But Haman's plan was obvious: He wanted to use Mordecai's execution to frighten the Jews and convince them that the king meant business when he approved the edict. The execution of a prominent Jew such as Mordecai would paralyze the wills of the Jewish people in the empire, and Haman would have them at his mercy.

There's another thing about this gallows that we're not sure of: Was it like the Western gallows, a device for hanging a person by the neck until dead? Or was it a stake on which a human body was impaled? The Persians were known for their cruel punishments, one of which was impaling live prisoners on sharp posts and leaving them there to suffer an agonizing death.

Whatever this gallows was, it turned out to be the instrument of Haman's own execution. God was standing in the shadows, keeping watch over His own.

"For the ways of man are before the eyes of the Lord, and

He ponders all his paths. His own iniquities entrap the wicked man, and he is caught in the cords of his sin. He shall die for lack of instruction, and in the greatness of his folly he shall go astray" (Prov. 5:21-23, NKJV).

T E N

Warning Signals

(In which God sounds an alarm,
but Haman won't listen)

You've probably seen the popular poster that reads: "Today is the first day of the rest of your life."

If anybody had said that to Haman as he left home early in the morning and hurried to the palace, they would have been wrong. They should have said, "Haman, today is the last day of your life!"

"As I live, saith the Lord God, I have no pleasure in the death of the wicked; but that the wicked turn from his way and live" (Ezek. 33:11, KJV).

"The Lord . . . is long-suffering toward us, not willing that any should perish but that all should come to repentance" (2 Peter 3:9, NKJV).

"O Jerusalem, Jerusalem, the one who kills the prophets and stones those who are sent to her! How often I wanted to gather your children together, as a hen gathers her chicks under her wings, but you were not willing!" (Matt. 23:37, NKJV)

On the basis of these three verses, we're safe in concluding that God's desire for sinners is not that they die but that they turn from their sins and be saved. There is joy in heaven when a sinner repents (Luke 15:7, 10), but the Lord won't force people to turn from their sins and trust His Son. "I wanted to . . . but you were not willing."

As much as we detest Haman and his foul deeds, we must keep in mind that God loves sinners and wants to save them. God is long-suffering and brings various influences to bear upon people's hearts as He seeks to turn them from their evil ways. We will see some of these influences at work in the events of this chapter.

1. A night of discovery (Es. 6:1-5)

Once again, we see the sovereign hand of God invisibly at work in the life of King Ahasuerus. God was working out His purposes whether the king knew it or not, and you can see in this paragraph at least five evidences of God's providence.

The king's insomnia (Es. 6:1a). "Uneasy lies the head that wears a crown," wrote Shakespeare. Solomon agreed: "The sleep of a laboring man is sweet, whether he eat little or much; but the abundance of the rich will not suffer him to sleep" (Ecc. 5:12, KJV). Was it the cares of state that kept the king awake? Was he worried about his finances? Did he eat and drink immoderately at the queen's feast? Or, was he puzzled about the queen's mysterious request?

Some or all of these worries may have played a part in the king's wakefulness, but behind them was the sovereign hand of the living God who watches over His people and never slumbers or sleeps (Ps. 121:3-4). God wanted the king to stay awake because He had something to tell him.

While visiting the zoo, I became fascinated with the "nocturnal exhibit." Here were animals that most of us never see because they sleep in the daytime and do their active living at night. "While you are resting," said one of the posters, "Nature is busily at work helping to keep the balance of life stable." I thought to myself, "While I'm asleep, my Heavenly Father is busily at work making sure the new day will be just what He wants it to be." God's compassions never fail but are "new every morning" (Lam. 3:22-23) because God never sleeps and never stops working all things together for our good (Rom. 8:28).

The king's choice of entertainment (Es. 6:1b). Ahasuerus wasn't at a loss for sources of entertainment! He could have called a concubine from the harem, or he might have brought in the court musicians to play for him. He and his guards could have played a game together, or he might have asked for a troubadour to entertain him with a ballad. His decision to have a book read to him was certainly of God.

Can God direct us even in such minor matters as our recreations? He certainly can. When I was a young Christian, my attendance at a friend's birthday party turned out to be one of the most important events in my life. Because of that evening, I made a decision about my educational plans. That decision eventually led to my changing schools and meeting the girl who became my wife. Never underestimate the extraordinary things God can do through an ordinary event like a birthday party.

The servant's choice of books (Es. 6:1c). God directed Ahasuerus to ask for the kingdom chronicles to be read to him. (That would put anybody to sleep!) But God also directed that the servant take from the shelf the very book that recorded Mordecai's service to the king five years before. Certainly there were other volumes available, but that's the one the servant selected.

Can God direct in the books that people pick up and read? Yes, He can. Late in February 1916, a British student bought a book at a used-book stall in a railway station. He had looked at that book and rejected it at least a dozen times before, but that day he purchased it. It was *Phantastes* by George Mac-Donald, and the reading of that book eventually led to that young man's conversion. Who was he? C.S. Lewis, perhaps the greatest and most popular apologist for the Christian faith of the middle-twentieth century. He wrote to a friend that he had picked up the book "by hazard," but I believe God had directed his choice.

God can even direct *what we read* in a book. A young man in North Africa sought peace, first in sensual pleasures and then in philosophy, but only became more miserable. One day he heard a neighbor child playing a game and saying, "Take it and read! Take it and read!" The young man immediately picked up the Scriptures and "happened" to open to Romans 13:13-14; and those verses brought him to faith in Christ. We know that young man today as Augustine, Bishop of Hippo, and author of numerous Christian classics.

The king's servant picked out the very book that told about Mordecai's good deed and read that section to Ahasuerus. How marvelous is the providence of God!

The king's delay in rewarding Mordecai (Es. 6:2-3). This is a key matter; for had Mordecai been honored five years before, the events of this critical day could not have occurred. Rewards and punishments were basic to the Persian system of maintaining loyalty, and it was unusual for meritorious service not to be rewarded. Then why was Mordecai's good deed written down but forgotten? Did some junior clerk in the bureaucracy have a grudge against Mordecai? Did an office memo go astray? We don't know; but this we do know, that God was in charge and already had the day selected for Mordecai to be honored.

Is God in charge of schedules? He certainly is! After befriending Pharaoh's butler, Joseph thought it would lead to his being released from prison; but Joseph had to wait two more years until the time God had chosen for him to become second ruler in Egypt (Gen. 40:23–41:1). God had a specific day selected for the Jews to leave Egypt (Ex. 12:40-42; see Gen. 15:13-16), and even the birth of Jesus Christ in Bethlehem occurred "when the fullness of the time was come" (Gal. 4:4, KJV). In the midst of a confused and troubled world, the dedicated believer is able to say, "My times are in Thy hand" (Ps. 31:15, KJV) and find peace in God's will.

It has often been said that "God's delays are not God's denials." We sometimes get impatient and wonder why the wicked are prospering while the righteous are suffering, but God is never in a hurry. He is long-suffering toward the wicked because He wants them to repent, and He is patient with His people because He wants them to receive the right reward at the right time for the right purpose. If Mordecai was ever puzzled because the king promoted Haman but ignored him, he would soon find out that God had not made a mistake.

The timely arrival of Haman (Es. 6:4). It's possible that Haman had been up all night, enjoying the supervision of the construction of the gallows on which he planned to hang (or impale) Mordecai. It was very early in the morning, but Haman wanted to see the king as soon as possible and get permission for the execution (Prov. 6:18). From Haman's point of view, the earlier the hanging, the better. Mordecai's body would be on exhibition all day, and this would delight Haman and also put fear into the hearts of the Jews in the city. After executing Mordecai, Haman could be certain that everybody would obey the king's command and bow down to him.

Suppose Haman had arrived two hours later? The king would have consulted with other advisers, and Haman would have been left out of the celebration for Mordecai. God wanted Haman to spend the day honoring Mordecai and not gloating over Mordecai's corpse on the gallows. God was actually warning Haman that he'd better change course or he would end up being destroyed.

When you review these evidences of the providence of

God, you can't help but want to praise and thank Him for the great God that He is. "The Lord brings the counsel of the nations to nothing; He makes the plans of the peoples of no effect. The counsel of the Lord stands forever, the plans of His heart to all generations" (Ps. 33:10-11, NKJV). "There is no wisdom, no insight, no plan that can succeed against the Lord" (Prov. 21:30, NIV). "If God be for us, who can be against us?" (Rom. 8:31, KJV)

2. A morning of decision (Es. 6:6-10)

It's one thing to enter the king's throne room, but now Haman was invited into the king's bedchamber. This new honor only increased Haman's pride and false confidence; he thought that he was in control of events and that Mordecai's doom was sealed. And when the king asked for Haman's advice on a personal matter, it inflated Haman's ego even more.

In verse 6, the king's question was vague and didn't identify "the man whom the king delights to honor" (NKJV). In his pride, Haman concluded that the king was speaking about him. After all, what other man in the empire deserved such honor from the king? After the way Mordecai had insulted him, Haman would now get double revenge: First Mordecai would see Haman honored by the king, and then Mordecai would be hanged on the gallows. Haman would then climax the day by feasting "merrily" (5:14) with the king and queen.

Little did proud Haman realize that, before the day would end, the situation would be completely reversed: Haman would be forced to honor Mordecai before all the people of the city; Esther's feast would turn out to be an exposé of the traitor; and Haman, not Mordecai, would end up on the gallows. "The righteous is delivered from trouble, and it comes to the wicked instead" (Prov. 11:8, NKJV).

"Before destruction the heart of a man is haughty, and

before honor is humility" (18:12, NKJV). The first half of that
verse applies to Haman and the last half to Mordecai. What a
difference a little comma makes! Proverbs 29:23 gives the
same message: "A man's pride shall bring him low, but the
humble in spirit will retain honor" (NKJV). On which side of
the comma do you live?

Thinking that the king was describing the honors he himself would receive, Haman asked for the very best: The man
to be honored should be dressed in the king's own apparel;
he should ride on the king's horse with the royal crest on its
head; and one of the noble princes should lead the horse
through the city and command the people to honor him. Such
an event would almost be like a coronation!

The more I ponder the character of Haman, the more con-
vinced I am that he wanted the throne for himself. As second
man in the empire, if anything happened to Ahasuerus, Haman was certainly in the best position to capture the throne
for himself. A proud man with selfish ambitions isn't content
to take second place if there's any possible way to secure
first place. If what is described in Esther 6:8-9 had actually
been done for Haman, it would have given the people of
Shushan the impression that Ahasuerus had chosen Haman
to be his successor.

Note that King Ahasuerus called Mordecai "the Jew" (v.
10). You get the impression that the king completely forgot
that he had permitted Haman to issue an edict to destroy the
Jews. One day the king is an enemy of the Jews, and a few
weeks later he honors one of the leading Jewish citizens! But
Ahasuerus had a debt to pay, for Mordecai had saved his life.
And perhaps in honoring Mordecai publicly, the king might
help calm the troubled citizens of the city (3:15).

It was a morning of decision. The king had decided to
reward Mordecai, and Haman had decided what the reward
should be. What were the results?

3. A day of disgrace (Es. 6:11-14)

We wonder what Haman's response was when the king told him to do all those things for Mordecai. Was he shocked? Did he show his astonishment openly? Probably not, because you didn't express yourself that freely before an Eastern monarch. With the practiced duplicity that got him where he was, Haman bowed to the king's commandment and obeyed.

First, he had to go out to the king's gate, get Mordecai, and bring him into the palace. Then he had to dress Mordecai in the king's robes. After putting Mordecai on the king's horse, Haman had to lead the horse throughout the city and proclaim, "This is what is done for the man the king delights to honor!" (v. 9, NIV) After he had visited all the city streets, Haman had to lead the horse back to the palace, remove the royal garments from Mordecai,[1] and send him back to his place at the city gate. What irony! For almost a whole day Haman was the servant of Mordecai, commanding the people to bow down and honor him! The thing Mordecai wouldn't do for Haman—bow down—Haman had to tell others to do for Mordecai!

How did this pageantry and prominence affect Mordecai? When it was over, he simply returned to his place at the gate and continued to serve the king. Applause doesn't change truly humble people, for their values are far deeper. God can trust His blessings with the humble because they seek to honor only the Lord.

Haman's reaction was quite different, for he was humiliated. He went home as soon as possible, his head covered as though he were grieving for the dead. This had been the way Mordecai had responded to the king's edict concerning the Jews (4:1-2). Again, the tables were turned.

---

[1]It's likely that Mordecai got to keep the garments since they had been worn by someone other than the king.

Even if they did bow down to him, Haman had no desire to see the public, because he had been humiliated before them and he knew that they were laughing at him behind his back. Such is the difference between reputation and character. Haman was a famous man, a man of reputation, only because the king had made him so; but he was not a man of character. His reputation depended on his office, his wealth, and his authority, all of which could easily be taken from him.

What a contrast between Haman's family gathering in 6:13 and the one recorded in 5:10-12! Whereas before, Haman had boasted of his greatness, now he had to confess how he had been humiliated. If there had been any other official on the horse but Mordecai the Jew, Haman might have been able to handle the situation; but having to give honor to a Jew demoralized Haman completely.

At this point, his wife and counselors made an interesting statement: "If Mordecai, before whom you have begun to fall, is of Jewish descent, you will not prevail against him but will surely fall before him" (6:13, NKJV). *His humiliation in the streets and these words in his house should have alarmed Haman and moved him to change his course of action. God was warning Haman, but the proud prime minister wouldn't heed the warning.* Had he sincerely repented and asked for mercy, it's likely that he could have saved his own life and the lives of his ten sons.

The Persians were a very superstitious people, and the advisers saw in the events of the day a "bad omen" for Haman's future. Perhaps they were also familiar with God's covenant with Abraham (Gen. 12:1-3), or maybe they just knew Jewish history. At any rate, they saw Haman falling from his place of prominence; and this dire prediction should have brought him to the place of humility and repentance.

While Haman was discussing his misfortunes with his wife and advisers, the king's eunuchs arrived at the door to escort

135

Haman to the queen's banquet. He had planned to go "merri-ly" to the feast, with Mordecai safely out of the way (5:14); but now everything had changed.

What would happen next? And what was the mysterious petition that Queen Esther would reveal at the banquet?

Off Haman went with the eunuchs to his last meal.

When God sounds the alarm, it pays to stop, look, and listen—and obey.

The Mask Comes Off

(In which Haman comes
to the end of his rope)

When they arrived at Esther's palace apartment, neither the king nor Haman knew that Esther was a Jewess. Haman was probably still distressed because of the events of the day, but he composed himself and hoped to enjoy the banquet. This is the seventh banquet recorded in the Book of Esther.

Had he known the nationality of the queen, Haman either would have run for his life or fallen on his face and begged the king for mercy. God had warned Haman through circumstances, through his advisers, and through his wife; but the prime minister would not heed the warnings. "The Lord detests all the proud of heart. Be sure of this: They will not go unpunished" (Prov. 16:5, NIV).

God's long-suffering led Haman into thinking he was safe. "Because sentence against an evil work is not executed speedily, therefore the heart of the sons of men is fully set in them to do evil" (Ecc. 8:11, NKJV). God's long-suffering today is an opportunity for people to repent (2 Peter 3:9), but our sinful world thinks it means God won't judge sinners at all. "For when they say, 'Peace and safety!' then sudden destruction comes upon them, as labor pains upon a pregnant woman. And they shall not escape" (1 Thes. 5:3, NKJV).

1. The queen's request (Es. 7:1-4)

Ever since the previous evening's banquet, Ahasuerus had been waiting to hear the queen's petition; so when the wine was served, he broached the subject. Of course, the statement "even to half of the kingdom" was a royal promise that wasn't to be taken literally (see 5:3; Dan. 5:16; Mark 6:23). It simply meant that the king would be generous. Therefore, tell him what you want.

During the previous twenty-four hours, Esther had probably rehearsed this speech many times; and now God gave her the strength to deliver it. Remember, she was taking her life in her hands, for if the king rejected her plea, that was the end.

She made it clear from the beginning that she depended on the favor of the king and wasn't trying to tell him what to do. She also said that her desire wasn't to please herself but to please the king. This was good psychology, especially when dealing with a chauvinistic monarch like Ahasuerus.

It was also wise on her part not to say, "There's a man in your kingdom who plans to destroy all of the Jews!" *She focused her petition on the fact that the queen's life was in danger and the king had to do something about it.* We have reason to believe Ahasuerus still loved his queen and didn't want any harm to come to her. As he sat there in her presence and beheld her beauty, her words moved him. What monster would want to kill the queen?

Not only was the queen's life in danger, but her people were also in danger of being slain. My guess is that this statement perplexed the king. Who were her people? Wasn't she a Persian? Has she been keeping a secret from me?

It was then that Esther reminded the king of the decree he had approved to wipe out the Jewish nation. In fact, her words are almost verbatim from the decree (Es. 3:13). Ahasuerus was smart enough to put two and two together and understand that Queen Esther was a Jewess, and he had unwittingly consented to her murder!

Esther continued by pointing out that the king had been paid to issue this decree (vv. 9-11). If he had sold the Jews as slaves, such a payment might have been just. But to sell them into death and total destruction was something for which nobody had enough money. "If it were only a matter of going into bondage," said Esther, "I would have kept quiet. Why bother the king with that? But wholesale murder is something I can't ignore."

Queen Esther bravely interceded for her people. How will the king respond? "Commit to the Lord whatever you do, and your plans will succeed. The Lord works out everything for His own ends—even the wicked for a day of disaster" (Prov. 16:3-4, NIV).

2. The king's rage (Es. 7:5-8)

At this point, try to imagine what was going through the mind of King Ahasuerus. Without openly accusing him, Esther has implicated the king in a horrible crime, and he was bound to feel guilty. The king knew that he had impetuously approved the decree. But he didn't realize that the decree was part of a conspiracy. He had signed the death warrant for his own wife! The king had to find a way to save his wife and save face at the same time.

In an absolute monarchy, the king is looked upon as a god and can do no wrong. This is why ancient monarchs always had a stable of scapegoats available—people who could take the blame for the ignorance or inefficiency of the throne. (Modern politicians often do the same thing.) Therefore, the king's question in verse 5 implied much more than, "Who is guilty?" The king was also looking for somebody to punish.

139

Ahasuerus had already received one surprise when he learned the nationality of his queen; and now he would be hit with another: His favorite officer was the adversary and enemy who had plotted the whole thing. Esther didn't reveal that Haman, like the king, had just learned from her own lips that she was a Jewess. Perhaps Ahasuerus concluded that Haman's crime was wanting to slay the queen and that he had decided to accomplish it by killing all the Jews. For that matter, maybe Haman was part of the Bigthan-Teresh conspiracy that Mordecai had exposed, a conspiracy to murder the king! (See 2:21-23.) *And like Esther, Mordecai was a Jew!*

Now we can better understand why God directed Esther to delay her pleas: He wanted to give Ahasuerus opportunity to learn what Mordecai had done, that Mordecai was a Jew and that he deserved to be honored. *If a Jew had saved the king's life, why should the king exterminate the Jews?*

"The king got up in a rage, left his wine and went out into the palace garden" (7:7, NIV). We've already noted that Ahasuerus was a man with a short temper (1:12); but on this occasion, his anger must have been volcanic. His masculine pride was hurt because he had misjudged the character of Haman. He had made a fool of himself by promoting Haman and by giving him so much influence. The king had also erred in approving the decree without first weighing all the facts (Prov. 18:13). As a result, he had endangered the lives of two very special Jews—Mordecai, who had saved his life, and Esther, his beloved wife.

No doubt the king walked to and fro in the garden, doing his best to control the anger that welled up within him. "The wrath of a king is as messengers of death" (Prov. 16:14, KJV). "The king's wrath is as the roaring of a lion" (19:12, KJV). No wonder Haman was afraid! He had been near enough to the king to recognize and interpret his every mood. He knew the king was about to become judge and jury and pass a sentence from which there was no escape.

But for Haman, there was one remote possibility: the mercy of the queen. Perhaps he could arouse her pity and get her to intercede for him. Esther knew Haman was a tool of the devil determined to destroy the Jewish people. Had he known originally that Esther was a Jewess, Haman might have cleverly worded the decree so that her life would be preserved; but he would still have had authority to annihilate all of her people. It was Haman's hatred for the queen's cousin Mordecai that started the whole conspiracy (Es. 3:5-6), and Esther wasn't about to abandon the one man who had meant so much to her.

In the Soncino Jewish commentary on Esther, Dr. S. Goldman makes this telling statement about 7:8: "The arrogant bully became, as usually in the face of disaster, a whining coward" *(The Five Megilloth,* p. 228). When the authority of the king had been behind him, Haman could courageously strut about, demand respect, and give orders. But now that the anger of the king was *against* him, Haman's true character was revealed. He was not a giant; he was only a midget full of pride and hot air! And all the king's horses and all the king's men couldn't put Haman's life back together again.

What a paradox! Haman had been furious because a Jewish *man* wouldn't bow down to him, and now Haman was prostrate before a Jewish *woman,* begging for his life! When the king entered the room and saw the scene, he accused Haman of trying to molest the queen. In his anger, the king would have exaggerated anything Haman did; and besides that, molesting the queen was a capital crime. Forget about the conspiracy; everybody could see for themselves that Haman was guilty of attacking the queen. For that crime alone, he deserved to die.

After escorting Mordecai around the city, Haman had covered *his head* in humiliation (6:12); but now the king's guards covered Haman's *face* in preparation for his execution. Had Haman covered his head in true humility and repentance, things would have been different, but he refused to listen to the warnings of the Lord. He was so controlled by pride and malice that he was blind to the dangers that laid ahead.

3. Haman's reward (Es. 7:9-10)

"The righteous is delivered from trouble, and it comes to the wicked instead" (Prov. 11:8, NKJV). The conspicuous gallows that Haman had constructed for Mordecai was convenient for the execution of Haman. Therefore, the king used it. Apparently Haman had let it be known in the palace that he planned to kill Mordecai, for the king's servant knew the purpose of the gallows. In his pride, Haman had boasted too much; and his words came back not only to haunt him but also to help slay him.

The day before, Haman had led Mordecai through the streets dressed in royal splendor; but now Haman was led through the streets with a covering over his face and a gallows at the end of the journey. Certainly Haman's wife Zeresh and their ten sons witnessed the execution, as did many of the Jews in the city. It must have given courage to the Jews to know that their enemy Haman was no longer on the scene.

"Do not be deceived: God cannot be mocked," warned Paul. "A man reaps what he sows" (Gal. 6:7, NIV). Haman sowed anger against Mordecai, and he reaped anger from the king. Haman wanted to kill Mordecai and the Jews, and the king killed Haman. "Even as I have seen, they that plow iniquity, and sow wickedness, reap the same" (Job 4:8, KJV). "He who sows wickedness reaps trouble" (Prov. 22:8, NIV).

This unchanging principle of sowing and reaping is illustrated throughout the Bible, *and it applies to both believers and unbelievers.* Jacob killed an animal and lied to his father, pretending to be Esau (Gen. 27:1-29); and years later Jacob's sons killed an animal and lied to him, pretending that Joseph was dead (37:31-35). Pharaoh gave orders to drown the Jewish baby boys (Ex. 1), and one day his army was drowned in the Red Sea (Ex. 14–15).

David secretly took his neighbor's wife and committed adultery (2 Sam. 11), and David's own son Absalom took his father's concubines and openly committed adultery with them (16:20-23). Furthermore, David's daughter Tamar was raped by her half brother Amnon (2 Sam. 13). David killed Bathsheba's husband (11:14-25), and three of David's own sons were slain: Absalom (2 Sam. 18), Amnon (13:23-36), and Adonijah (1 Kings 2:13-25). Saul of Tarsus encouraged the stoning of Stephen (Acts 8:1); and when he became Paul the missionary, he was stoned at Lystra (14:19-20).

But let's keep in mind that this law of sowing and reaping also applies to doing what is good and right. If we sow to the flesh, we reap corruption; but if we sow to the Spirit, we reap life everlasting (Gal. 6:8). No good deed done for the glory of Jesus Christ will ever be forgotten before God. No loving word spoken in Jesus' name will ever be wasted. If we don't see the harvest in this life, we'll see it when we stand before the Lord. Even a cup of cold water given in the name of Christ will have its just reward (Matt. 10:42; 25:31-46).

Haman was hanged, or impaled, on his own gallows, and his body taken down and buried. *All of Haman's wealth and glory couldn't rescue him from death nor could he take any of it with him.* "Those who trust in their wealth and boast in the multitude of their riches, none of them can by any means redeem his brother, nor give to God a ransom for him — for the redemption of their souls is costly. . . . Do not be afraid when one becomes rich, when the glory of his house is increased; for when he dies he shall carry nothing away; his glory shall not descend after him" (Ps. 49:6-8, 16-17, NKJV).

143

In 1 Peter 1:18-19, Peter tells us how costly our redemption is: the shedding of the blood of Jesus Christ, the Son of God.

Not only is there a personal lesson here, but there is also a lesson about the nation of Israel: *Every enemy that has ever tried to destroy Israel has been destroyed.* "I will bless those who bless you, and I will curse him who curses you" is God's promise to Israel (Gen. 12:3, NKJV), and He has always kept it. God takes His promises seriously even if the nations of the world ignore them or challenge them.

This doesn't mean that God necessarily approves everything Israel has done or will do, but it does mean that God doesn't approve of those who try to destroy His chosen people. Whether it's Pharaoh in Egypt, Nebuchadnezzar in Babylon, Haman in Persia, or Hitler in Germany, the enemy of the Jews is the enemy of Almighty God and will not succeed.

"Then was the king's wrath pacified" (Es. 7:10, KJV). The Hebrew word translated "pacified" is used in Genesis 8:1 to describe the receding waters of the Flood. The king's anger had welled up within him and reached its peak when he executed Haman. Now it subsided, and the king was himself again. But though the adversary was out of the way, the problem was not completely solved; for the king's decree was still in effect *and could not be changed.* It was now the third month (Es. 8:9), and there were nine months to go before the fateful day when the Jews could legally be slain (3:13).

How would Esther and Mordecai solve this problem?

That is the topic of the next chapter.

ESTHER 8

From Victims to Victors

(In which the good news of a new law
brings hope and joy)

Haman was dead, but his murderous edict was still very much alive. Long after wicked people are gone, the consequences of their evil words and deeds live on. Even today, innocent people are suffering because of guilty people who lie in their graves.

Unless something intervened, within nine months the Persians would attack the Jews and wipe them off the face of the earth. There were about 15 million Jews among the estimated 100 million people in the empire. Therefore, the odds were definitely against God's people. Of course, God's people have always been a minority; and "one with God is a majority." The Lord had brought Esther and Mordecai to the kingdom "for such a time as this," and they were prepared to act.

1. The promotion of Mordecai (Es. 8:1-2, 15)

According to the ancient historians, whenever a traitor was executed, the throne appropriated his property. Had Ahasuerus confiscated Haman's property for himself, he would have acquired a great deal of wealth; but he chose to give Haman's estate to Esther. More than an act of generosity, this gift was probably the king's way of atoning for his foolish decisions

145

that had brought so much pain to Esther and her people. It's possible that Esther later shared some of this great wealth with the Jews so they could prepare themselves for the coming crisis.

Ahasuerus knew that both Esther and Mordecai were Jews, but now he was to learn that they were also cousins. Ahasuerus and Mordecai were relatives by marriage! When Haman was deposed, the king took back his royal ring (3:10), the insignia of the authority of the throne (8:8, 10; 3:12), and he gave the ring to Mordecai, making him prime minister. With a Jewish queen and a Jewish prime minister in the palace, the Jews in the empire were in a better political position than ever before.

Esther gave the management of Haman's vast estate into the hands of Mordecai, who had first opposed Haman and refused to bow down. Were it not for Mordecai's courage and encouragement of Esther, Haman would still be in control. "Wait on the Lord, and keep His way, and He shall exalt you to inherit the land; when the wicked are cut off, you shall see it. I have seen the wicked in great power, and spreading himself like a native green tree. Yet he passed away, and behold, he was no more" (Ps. 37:34-36, NKJV).

The king made sure that Mordecai had a uniform worthy of his office, and it's described in Esther 8:15. No longer did Mordecai wear old borrowed robes (6:7-11) but new robes prepared especially for him. The official royal colors were blue and white (see 1:6). The golden "crown" was probably a large turban which, along with the robe of white and purple, identified Mordecai as an important man of great authority.

Everything that Haman had acquired from the king by his scheming, Mordecai received as gifts, because Mordecai was a deserving man. At the beginning of this story, Esther and Mordecai were hardly exemplary in the way they practiced their religious faith; but now we get the impression that things have changed. Both of them have affirmed their Jewish nationality and both were the means of calling all the Jews in the empire to prayer and fasting. In one sense, they spearheaded a Jewish "revival" and made being Jewish a more honorable thing in the empire.

God doesn't always give this kind of a "happy ending" to everybody's story. Today, not all faithful Christians are promoted and given special honors. Some of them get fired because of their stand for Christ! God hasn't promised that we'll be promoted and made rich, but He has assured us that He's in control of all circumstances and that He will write the last chapter of the story. If God doesn't promote us here on earth, He certainly will when we get to glory.

2. Esther's petition (Es. 8:3-6)

Wealth, prestige, and personal security could never satisfy Esther so long as her people were still in danger. To her, the most important thing in life was not her comfort but their deliverance; and she couldn't rest until the matter was settled. How unlike some believers today who ignore the needs of a lost world while they search for new ways to spend money and have fun! They think that attending church and bringing their offerings fulfills their Christian responsibilities and gives them the freedom to do whatever they please with the rest of their time and money. We need more people like Esther whose burden for condemned people was greater than any other thing in her life.

Years ago, in a Youth for Christ late-night prayer meeting, I heard attorney Jacob Stam pray, "Lord, the only thing most of us know about sacrifice is how to spell the word." I never forgot that statement, and I confess that it sometimes still haunts me. I recall another YFC staff meeting at which the late Bill Carle sang "So Send I You," and the Spirit of God brought all of us to our knees in prayer with a new dedication to help reach the world for Christ.

Esther couldn't do everything, but she could do something; and what she could do, she did. She approached the throne of the king and asked him to reverse the edict that Haman had devised. *It was her interceding at the throne that saved the people of Israel from slaughter.* She was asking nothing for herself, except that the king save her people and deliver her from the heavy burden on her heart.

As I've studied the Scriptures, I've been impressed with the many people who have prayed for the Jews. When Israel sinned, Moses met God on the mountain and interceded for them (Ex. 32). He was even willing for God to blot him out of the Book of Life if that's what it took to rescue the nation. Centuries later, the Apostle Paul said he was willing to be "accursed from Christ" if it would help save unbelieving Israel (Rom. 9:1-3, KJV).

On Mount Carmel, Elijah prayed for disobedient Israel (1 Kings 18); and in the palace, Nehemiah prayed for the Jews in Jerusalem (Neh. 1). Like Nehemiah, Ezra wept and prayed and asked God to help His sinful people (Ezra 9); and Daniel humbled himself and fasted and prayed that he might understand what God's plan was for Israel (Dan. 9). "I have set watchmen on your walls, O Jerusalem, who shall never hold their peace day or night. You who make mention of the Lord, do not keep silent, and give Him no rest till He establishes and till He makes Jerusalem a praise in the earth" (Isa. 62:6-7, NKJV).

"Pray for the peace of Jerusalem; they shall prosper who love thee" (Ps. 122:6, KJV). There can be no peace in this world until there is peace in Jerusalem, and there can be no peace in Jerusalem unless God's people obey this command and pray, "Thy kingdom come."

"It was a master stroke of the Devil when he got the church and the ministry so generally to lay aside the mighty weapon of prayer," wrote evangelist R.A. Torrey in *How to Obtain Fullness of Power in Christian Life and Service.* "The Devil is perfectly willing that the church should multiply its organizations and its deftly-contrived machinery for the conquest of the world for Christ, if it will only give up praying" *(Sword of the Lord* reprint, p. 59).

Esther's example encourages us to come to God's throne and intercede on behalf of others, especially the nations of the world where lost souls need to be delivered from death. *One concerned person devoted to prayer can make a great difference in this world, for prayer is the key that releases the power of God.* "Yet you do not have because you do not ask" (James 4:2, NKJV).

3. The king's proclamation (Es. 8:7-17)

The problem Esther and Mordecai faced was that the king, simply by executive fiat, couldn't cancel the first edict since the laws of the Medes and Persians were unalterable. In modern democratic nations, legislatures can reverse decisions and revoke laws, and the supreme court of the land can even declare laws unconstitutional; but not so in the ancient despotic Persian Empire. The voice of the king was the law of the land, and the king could do no wrong.

The king couldn't legally revoke his edict, but he could issue a new decree that would favor the Jews. The new decree would let everybody in the empire know that the king wanted his people to have a different attitude toward the Jews and look favorably upon them. The citizens didn't have to hire a lawyer to explain the new edict to them. You can be sure they got the message: Don't attack the Jews on March 7.

Since Mordecai was now prime minister, it was his job to draft the new decree. What he did was give the Jews permission to defend themselves against anybody who tried to kill them and take their property. There were many people in the empire like Haman, who hated the Jews, wanted to destroy them, and get their hands on their wealth. The new decree allowed the Jews to assemble and defend themselves, but they were not allowed to be the aggressors.

Scholars don't agree on the translation of verse 11. The *Authorized Version* gives the impression that the edict allowed the Jews to destroy the wives and children of their attackers and plunder their spoil, and the NASB seems to agree with this interpretaion. The NIV connects "women and children" with the Jews being attacked and doesn't suggest that the Jews killed the women and children of their attackers. I prefer the NIV translation.

If you read 3:11-13, you will see the similarity of the wording of the two decrees. Mordecai used the "official language" of the government, because legal statements must be expressed in legal language. This language may seem strange to outsiders, but without it we would have confusion and misinterpretation. You can't write the law the way you write a poem or a recipe.

According to 8:9, the new edict was written on the twenty-third day of the third month, which on our calendar would be June 25, 474 B.C. (Remember, the Jewish calendar begins with the month of April.) The first decree was issued on April 17 (3:12). Thus, about seventy days had passed since Haman had declared war on the Jews. "D Day" for the Jews was March 7 (3:13). Therefore, the people had about eight months to get ready.

We must pause and consider whether it was really ethical for Mordecai to give the Jews the authority to kill and loot. People who deny the divine inspiration of the Bible like to point to the various "massacres" in Scripture as evidence that the God of the Bible is "a bully." Imagine worshiping a god that commanded the slaughter of whole populations!

First, let's consider the edict that Ahasuerus issued, *for that's where all the trouble started.* If it was wicked for Mordecai to tell the Jews to defend themselves, then it was even more wicked for Haman and Ahasuerus to tell the Persians to attack the Jews in the first place! Self-defense isn't a crime, but genocide definitely is. Do these critics approve of the *king's* edict? I certainly hope not! Well, if they don't approve of the king's decree, which permitted murder, then how can they disapprove of Mordecai's decree, which allowed the Jews the right to defend themselves? Better that Haman's decree had never been issued; but since it was published, better that Mordecai disarmed it by issuing his decree.

Now, let's look at the record in chapter 9, where you discover three important facts: The Jews killed only those who attacked them; they killed only the men (9:6, 12, 15); and they didn't lay hands on the loot, although they had the right to do so (vv. 10, 15-16). The fact that the Jews killed 800 men in the city of Shushan alone (vv. 6, 15) proves that there were many Persians just waiting for the opportunity to attack God's people. (It's estimated that there were probably half a million people in the capital city.)

The total number of the slain was 75,000 (v. 16) out of a population of perhaps 100 million people. But the fact that more than 75,000 people were prepared to slaughter *defenseless* Jews shows how many of the king's people hated God's people. And the fact that these people were even willing to attack *when they knew the Jews would protect themselves* is proof that anti-Semitism was very strong throughout the empire. The critics say it was wrong for the Jews to kill 75,000 would-be murderers. Would it have been better if the 75,000 Persians had killed ten times as many Jews?

Mordecai's decree was in complete harmony with God's covenant with Abraham: "I will bless those who bless you, and I will curse him who curses you" (Gen. 12:3, NKJV). Isaac

151

also would have agreed with Mordecai; for when Isaac blessed Jacob, he said, "Cursed be everyone who curses you, and blessed be those who bless you" (27:29, NKJV). In addition, God promised Moses, "I will be an enemy to your enemies and an adversary to your adversaries" (Ex. 23:22, NKJV). And don't forget that quotation from Dr. J. Vernon McGee: "The Jew has attended the funeral of every one of the nations that tried to exterminate him."

It's one thing to write a liberating new edict and quite another thing to get the message out to the people. Mordecai put the secretaries to work translating and copying the decree, and then he sent the couriers to carry the good news to the people in the various provinces of the empire. The couriers "hastened" because they were "pressed on by the king's commandment" (Es. 8:14, KJV). The NIV translates it "spurred on by the king's command."

If only the church today were like those secretaries and couriers! How we need to tell the peoples of the world in their own languages the good news of salvation through faith in Jesus Christ! The King has commanded us, and we must go, but for some reason we linger. If a group of pagan scribes and messengers, without modern means of transportation and communication, could take Mordecai's decree to an entire empire, how much more should Christian workers be able to take Christ's Gospel to a lost world!

Ever since the fall of Adam, "the law of sin and of death" has been in force in this world (Rom. 8:2; 5:12-21); *and God will not rescind that law.* The wages of sin is still death (Rom. 6:23). Through the death and resurrection of Jesus Christ, God put another law into effect, "the law of the Spirit of life in Christ Jesus" (8:2). God obeyed the law of sin and death when He gave His Son Jesus to bear our sins and die on the cross. But then God raised Him from the dead and put a new decree into effect that makes it possible for sinners to be saved. Now He wants us to put that good news into every tongue and take that good news to every nation.

This chapter begins with Queen Esther in tears (Es. 8:3), but it ends with the Jews rejoicing and feasting (vv. 15-17). Happiness of one kind or another is mentioned in this paragraph at least seven times. (This is the eighth feast mentioned in the Book of Esther.) The Jews had been mourning and fasting, but now they were ecstatic with joy.

The thing that made the difference was not the *writing* of the decree or even its *distribution* in the various provinces. The thing that made the difference was the fact that *the Jews believed the decree.* It was their faith in Mordecai's word that changed their lives. They had hope, joy, and peace because they had faith in what the prime minister said. "Now may the God of hope fill you with all joy and peace in believing, that you may abound in hope by the power of the Holy Spirit" (Rom. 15:13, NKJV).

The statement that "many of the people of the land became Jews" (Es. 8:17, KJV) is variously interpreted. The obvious meaning is that many Gentiles in the empire forsook their pagan religions and became Jewish proselytes. But since the Jews were far from Jerusalem and the ministry of the priests, these "converts" couldn't be initiated fully into the Jewish faith. They became what were known later as "God-fearers" or "worshipers of God" (Acts 10:2; 16:14; 18:7).

I think the phrase means that many of the Gentiles in the empire sided with the Jews and acted as though they were Jews. They weren't ashamed to be identified with the Jews even though the Jews had enemies.

After President Reagan was shot, when he was being prepared for surgery, he jokingly said to the medical team, "I hope all of you are Republicans." One of the doctors replied, "Mr. President, today *all* of us are Republicans." That was the attitude of many of the people in the Persian Empire when Mordecai's edict was published: "Today, *all* of us are Jews."

The Book of Esther opens with the Jews keeping a very low profile, so much so that Esther and Mordecai wouldn't even confess their nationality. But now the Jews are proud of their race and so happy with what God had done that they were attracting others to their faith! Even the pagan Gentiles could see that God was caring for His people in a remarkable way.

Evangelist Billy Sunday said, "If you have no joy in your religion, there's a leak in your Christianity somewhere." If Christian believers today manifested more of the joy of the Lord, perhaps those outside the faith would be attracted to the church and be willing to consider the message of the Gospel.

It's worth trying.

God Keeps His Promises

(In which the tables are turned,
and then the tables are spread)

Seek the peace of the city where I have caused you to be carried away captive." That was God's counsel to the Jews through the Prophet Jeremiah (Jer. 29:7, NKJV); and for the most part, they obeyed it. It wasn't the Jews who had declared war on the Gentiles, but the Gentiles who had declared war on the Jews!

"D Day" arrived for the Jews, the day appointed by Haman's decree for the slaughter of God's chosen people in the empire. But Mordecai's decree had changed that "D" from "destruction" to "deliverance." The Jews had permission to resist their enemies and had been given nine months to prepare for the encounter. The people in the empire who hated the Jews were hoping for victory, but "the tables were turned and the Jews got the upper hand over those who hated them" (Es. 9:1, NIV).

1. Vindication: the fear of the Jews (Es. 9:1-16)

The Jewish men were organized and armed, ready to meet any enemy who would attack them and their families and try to take their possessions. But the Lord had given them a greater weapon than their swords, because "the fear of the

Jews fell upon them" (8:17, KJV; 9:2). This was a fear that God had sent into the hearts of the Gentiles to keep them from fighting His people.

This reminds us of the experience of Jacob as he traveled from Shechem to Bethel. "And they journeyed: and the terror of God was upon the cities that were round about them, and they did not pursue after the sons of Jacob" (Gen. 35:5, KJV). It was this same fear that went before Israel as they entered the Promised Land. "This day I will begin to put the dread and fear of you upon the nations under the whole heaven, who shall hear the report of you, and shall tremble and be in anguish because of you" (Deut. 2:25, NKJV, and see 11:25). Rahab told the two Jewish spies that the fear of Israel had paralyzed the nations in Canaan (Josh. 2:8-11; 5:1; 9:24), and that fear helped give Israel the victory.

One of the problems with our world today is that "there is no fear of God before their eyes" (Rom. 3:18, KJV). Like Pharaoh, people are saying, "Who is the Lord, that I should obey His voice?" (Ex. 5:2, KJV) *But have they seen anything in the people of God that would make them want to fear the Lord?* Is there such devotion to God among God's people that an outsider attending one of our meetings would fall down on his face, worship God, and "report that God is truly among you"? (1 Cor. 14:25, NKJV)

The fear of God protects those who fear God and believe His promises. Because the Jews believed Mordecai's decree, they had new courage and were not afraid of the enemy; and their courage put fear into the hearts of the enemy. (See Phil. 1:28.) Before King Jehoshaphat went out to battle, God's message to him was: "Believe in the Lord your God, and you shall be established; believe His prophets, and you shall prosper" (2 Chron. 20:20). That is still wise counsel.

But there was another aspect to this fear that helped give the Jews their victory, and that was the people's fear of Mordecai (Es. 9:3). The princes, deputies, governors, and officers of the king throughout the empire were in such awe of Mordecai that they even helped the Jews defend themselves against the Persians. God had given Mordecai his high position and his great reputation, and Mordecai used his authority to do the will of God.

Christians today who live in a democratic pluralistic society can't get into political office in order to use that office to promote their own religious faith and destroy those who disagree with them. Mordecai was prime minister in a government where his word was law. Christians today, however, can so live their faith that the power of God is seen in their lives, and the enemy will think twice before attacking. And yet, instead of the godless world being afraid of the church, the church is afraid of the world *and so imitates the world that it's difficult to tell the difference between the two.*

The church today is no longer "fair as the moon, clear as the sun, and terrible as an army with banners" (Song 6:10, KJV). Rather, we are "wretched, and miserable, and poor, and blind, and naked" (Rev. 3:17, KJV), which is the description of prisoners of war. Instead of being the conquerors, we're the prisoners! No wonder the world has no fear of the Lord.

"For though we live in the world, we do not wage war as the world does. The weapons we fight with are not the weapons of the world" (2 Cor. 10:3-4, NIV). Whenever the church has tried to use the weapons of this world to fight its battles, the consequences have been embarrassing if not disastrous. Wearing the whole armor of God (Eph. 6:10ff), however, and depending on prayer and the Word of God (Acts 6:4), the Christian soldier can march forward with courage and faith.

The Persians who attacked the Jews were actually cooperating with Haman, an Amalekite; and this made them the enemies of God (Es. 9:5). In slaying those who attacked them, the Jews were only doing to the enemy what King Saul had refused to do (1 Sam. 15).

In Esther 9:5-15, we're given the report from Shushan; and, in verses 16-17, additional news is given about what happened in the other parts of the empire. During two days of conflict, the Jews killed 800 of their enemies in Susa alone (vv. 6, 15). It's remarkable that so many Persians would have dared to attack the Jews right in the king's own city where both Esther and Mordecai lived. Perhaps these people had been loyal to Haman and dependent on his bounty. Now they were angry because their hero had fallen and his wealth was gone.

Since the Jews were not the aggressors, it means that the ten sons of Haman had taken up arms and attacked the Jews; and all ten of them were slain. The bodies of the ten sons were hanged on Haman's gallows as a warning to the enemy. (In the text of the Hebrew Scriptures, the ten names are arranged on the page to look like a gallows. On the Feast of Purim, the synagogue reader reads these ten names all in one breath because the sons of Haman all died together.) The sight of ten corpses on Haman's gallows would certainly deter the Persians from attacking the Jews and would result in the saving of lives.

Some commentators have seen Esther's request in verses 12-13 as evidence of a vindictive spirit on her part, but this was not the case. Haman's strongest support was in the capital city where people had bowed down to him and benefited from his favors. Since it would be easy for them to get together and plan their strategy, Esther wanted to be sure that none of them would survive to cause further trouble. Perhaps she had received private intelligence that Haman's supporters had planned to attack again the next day, prompting her to ask Ahasuerus for permission to extend the Jews' right to defend themselves.

The Jews in the other parts of the empire killed 75,000 in

one day, which shows how many people hated the Jews and wanted to destroy them. It averages out to about 600 per province. Since the Jews were greatly outnumbered in the empire, their victory was certainly a tribute to their faith and courage.

Three times in the record it's stated that the Jews didn't take any of the spoil (vv. 10, 15-16). It was in taking spoil from the enemy that King Saul lost his kingdom (1 Sam. 15:12-23), and the Jews didn't repeat his mistake. They were not out after wealth. They wanted only to protect themselves and vindicate their right to live safely in the empire. And remember, the Jews killed only those who first attacked them; the Jews were not the aggressors.

2. Celebration: the feast of the Jews (Es. 9:17-32)

It's sad when a nation (or a church) forgets its heroes and the providential events that have kept it alive. How easy it is for a new generation to come along and take for granted the blessings that previous generations struggled and sacrificed to attain! The Jews didn't make that mistake but established the Feast of Purim to remind their children year after year that God had saved Israel from destruction.

While Purim is not a Christian festival, Christians certainly ought to rejoice with their Jewish friends because every spiritual blessing we have has come through the Jews. The Jews gave to the world the knowledge of the true and living God, the Scriptures, and the Savior. The first Christians were Jewish believers, and so were the first missionaries. Jesus was a Jew who died on Passover, a Jewish feast day, and rose again from the dead on another Jewish holy day, the Feast of Firstfruits. The Holy Spirit came from heaven upon a group of Jewish believers on a Jewish holiday, Pentecost. "Salvation is from the Jews" (John 4:22). If there had been no Jews, there would be no church.

There's nothing wrong with *meaningful* tradition. The church is always one generation short of extinction; and if we don't pass on to our children and grandchildren what God has done for us and our fathers, the church will die of apathy and ignorance. "Come, my children, listen to me; I will teach you the fear of the Lord" (Ps. 34:11, NIV). It's when tradition gradually becomes *traditionalism* that we get into trouble. Theologian Jaroslav Pelikan said, "Tradition is the living faith of the dead; traditionalism is the dead faith of the living."

The Jews in the provinces finished their fighting on the thirteenth day of Adar (March) and spent the next day celebrating. But since the Jews in Shushan were still defending themselves on the fourteenth day, they didn't get to celebrate until the fifteenth. In the beginning, the Jews were united in their victory but divided in their celebration. It all depended on whether you lived in the city or the country. Mordecai, however, later issued a letter that instructed all the Jews to celebrate on both the fourteenth and fifteenth days of the month (Es. 9:20-22).

Today, the Jews begin their celebration with a fast on the thirteenth day of the month (v. 31), commemorating the date on which Haman's evil decree was issued (3:12). They go to the synagogue and hear the Book of Esther publicly read; and whenever the name of Haman is mentioned, they cry out, "May he be accursed!" or "May his name perish!" Children bring a special Purim rattle called a "gregar" and use it to make noise every time they hear Haman's name read.

On the morning of the fourteenth day of the month, the Jews again go to the synagogue, where the Esther story is read again and the congregation engages in prayer. The story about Moses and the Amalekites (Ex. 17:8-16) is also read. Then the celebrants go home to a festive holiday meal with gifts and special foods, and the celebrating continues on the next day. They also send gifts and food to the poor and needy so that everybody can rejoice together.

The name "Purim" is the plural of the Babylonian word *pur* which means "lot." It originates from Haman's casting of lots to determine the day when the Jews would be destroyed (Es. 9:24; 3:7). Even though there was no divine sanction given to this new feast, the Jews determined that it would be celebrated from generation to generation (9:26-28). Note the emphasis on teaching the children the meaning of Purim so that the message of the feast would not be lost in future generations.

There is a godly patriotism that goes beyond mere nationalism and civic pride and gives glory to God for what He has done. To see the hand of God in history and praise God for His goodness and mercy, and to ask God to forgive us for our sins, is perhaps the best way for the Christian patriot to celebrate a national holiday. But dedication must follow celebration. The American political leader Adlai Stevenson said, "Patriotism is not short, frenzied outbursts of emotion, but the tranquil and steady dedication of a lifetime."

Not only did Mordecai the prime minister send a letter of instruction to the Jews in the empire, but Esther the queen also joined Mordecai in sending a second letter (vv. 29-32). Perhaps some of the Jews in the provinces didn't want to change from their original day of celebration (v. 19), and it was necessary for both the queen and prime minister to issue this second letter to keep peace in the nation. Too often God's people defeat the enemy and then celebrate the victory by fighting among themselves!

This second letter is described as "words of peace and truth" (v. 30), which suggests that there was a division among the Jewish people that needed to be healed. Not only did Esther and Mordecai send letters, but they also had the matter written into the book (diary?) that Mordecai used as his personal record (vv. 20, 32). It's possible that this book became a part of the official records of the empire.

The story of the victory of the Jews over their enemies was celebrated in an annual feast, recorded in two official letters, written in a journal, and ultimately included in the Old Testament Scriptures! What a rebuke to our modern "throw-away society" that has forgotten history and, like the Athenians of old, spends its time "in nothing else, but either to tell, or to hear some new thing" (Acts 17:21, KJV). Philosopher George Santayana was right when he said, "Those who do not remember the past are condemned to relive it."

3. Exaltation: the fame of Mordecai (Es. 10:1-3)

This brief chapter tells us that Mordecai, unlike his predecessor Haman, used his office to serve the king and help the Jews. Sometimes when people are elevated to high office, they forget their roots and ignore the needs of the common people. Mordecai wasn't that kind of man. Even though his political deeds are recorded in the official annals of the empire, what he did for his people has been recorded by the Lord and will be rewarded.

Why did the author mention the new tax program of King Ahasuerus? What does this have to do with Mordecai and the Jews? Some Bible students think that it was Mordecai who engineered this new system of tribute *as a substitute for war and plunder as a source of kingdom wealth.* Now that there was peace in the kingdom, the Jews were free to work, earn money, and prosper; and the prosperity of the Jews increased the prosperity of the empire in general. Mordecai reminded the king that the throne deserved a share in that prosperity. After all, it was the king who had chosen Esther, a Jewess, and promoted Mordecai, a Jew; and all three of them had worked together to save the Jews from destruction. Didn't the people of the empire, Jews and Gentiles alike, have an obligation to their monarch?

But the important message in this chapter is that God continued to use Mordecai to help the Jewish people. The Jews were aliens in a foreign land and subject to all kinds of harassment and abuse. Mordecai saw to it that they were treated with fairness. The last words of the book are variously translated. The *Authorized Version* says "and speaking peace to all his seed," suggesting that he encouraged the Jews and kept them at peace with one another. The NIV reads "and spoke up for the welfare of all the Jews." This implies that there were still forces at work in the empire opposing and threatening the Jews, but Mordecai represented them at court and protected them. "He did his best for his people, and was a friend at court for all of them" (TLB).

The exciting drama of Esther is over, but the blessings go right on. God preserved the Jewish nation so that we today can have a Bible and a Savior. Now it's our job to tell the whole world about this Savior and seek to win as many as we can to the Lord. We are the King's couriers, and we dare not fail.

Ruth and Esther reach across the centuries, join hands, and say to the church today: BE COMMITTED!

Chapter One

You Can't Run Away
(Ruth 1)

1. What three mistakes to avoid are illustrated in the experiences of Naomi and her husband?

2. "When trouble comes to our lives, we can endure it, escape it, or enlist it." Explain each option.

3. What reasons or circumstances might cause us to run from our problems as Naomi and Elimelech did?

4. What was wrong with Naomi's decision to go back to Bethlehem?

5. Why do you think Ruth was so determined to go with Naomi?

6. How did God demonstrate His grace in Ruth's life?

7. How did Naomi react to her problems?

8. Do you think Naomi was exaggerating her situation? Did she have any reason to be thankful?

9. What happens to Christians when they concentrate more on themselves and their problems than on God?

10. What experiences have you had in starting over as Ruth and Naomi did?

Chapter Two

The Greatest of These
(Ruth 2)

1. How did Ruth demonstrate her faith in God in Bethlehem?

2. "When we commit our lives to the Lord, what happens to us happens by way of appointment and not by accident." Do you agree? Give examples from your life.

3. How was Ruth's response to Boaz an example for Christians to follow in their response to Jesus?

4. What caused the positive change in Naomi's attitude?

5. What reasons do you have to "rejoice in hope"?

6. How is the Christian's hope different from the hope that the world clings to?

7. "One person, trusting the Lord and obeying His will, can change a situation from defeat to victory." Can you think of examples (biblical and contemporary) of this truth?

8. "Grace is love that pays the price to help the undeserving one." What does that mean to you?

9. What obstacles to faith did Ruth have to overcome?

10. What was an important turning point in your life? Describe it.

Chapter Three

The Midnight Meeting
(Ruth 3)

1. "It's when we serve others that we ourselves receive the greatest joy and satisfaction." Do you agree? Share personal experiences.

2. How was Ruth washing herself before she went to meet Boaz a picture of what we must do to have a deeper relationship with the Lord?

3. Do you agree that "if God were to take the Holy Spirit out of this world, much of what the church is doing would go right on; and nobody would know the difference"? Explain.

4. Why can't we come into God's presence clothed in our own righteousness? What do we need instead?

5. "The will of God is not a cafeteria where we can pick and choose what we want." What does that mean to you?

6. How does God give us assurance today?

7. How did God obey His own law when He accomplished our salvation in Christ?

8. Do you have trouble waiting for God to work? How do you control your impatience?

9. What does Psalm 46:10 mean to you?

10. Do you believe that Jesus is working unceasingly for you? How is He working in you?

Chapter Four

Love Finds a Way
(Ruth 4)

1. What does redemption mean?

2. How is Boaz, the kinsman redeemer, a picture of Christ?

3. What are some similarities between Ruth, the bride of Boaz, and the church, the bride of Christ?

4. How did God use Ruth and Boaz's baby, Obed, to be a source of blessing to many?

5. What was the greatest thing God ever did for David?

6. How does God's treatment of Ruth show His grace and power?

7. Think of the commitment spelled out in traditional wedding vows. How does that compare with your commitment to Christ?

8. Ruth left behind an eternal legacy. What legacy would you like to leave for your family?

9. "For a Christian, God still writes the last chapter." What does that mean to you?

10. What has the Book of Ruth taught you about deepening your relationship with the Lord?

Chapter Five

The Queen Says, "No!"
(Esther 1)

1. What were the king's weaknesses?

2. Can you think of other Bible characters who had too much pride?

3. How may pride be a problem in the Christian's life?

4. How can we get rid of pride and boastfulness?

5. What do you think a Christian's attitude should be about drinking?

6. "We must be careful that our anger at sin doesn't become sinful anger." What does that mean to you?

7. "When the ego is pricked, it releases a powerful poison that makes people do all sorts of things they'd never do if they were humble and submitted to the Lord." Do you agree? Explain.

8. The king's counselors, when consulted about the queen's disobedience, made a mountain out of a molehill. Do you ever overreact to small problems that way?

9. What does the king's experience teach us about who we should go to for advice?

10. Though God is not mentioned in the Book of Esther, how can we see Him working?

Chapter Six

The New Queen
(Esther 2)

1. "God is never surprised by circumstances or at a loss for prepared servants." Do you agree?

2. What three evidences of God's hand at work do you see in this chapter of Esther?

3. Do ungodly leaders of nations thwart God's plans? Explain.

4. Why do you think Esther and Mordecai concealed their identity as Jews?

5. Why do you think the king was more attracted to Esther than to all the other women brought to him?

6. Do you think Mordecai was a "secret disciple" like Nicodemus or just neglectful of honoring God publicly? Explain.

7. Do you think Mordecai and Esther understood that God was putting them where He could use them? Explain.

8. "God's timing is always perfect, and He sees to it that no good deed is ever wasted." What examples have you seen of this?

9. How can faith in God's sovereignty impact our everyday living?

10. It's obvious that God uses ordinary, imperfect people. How do you think He wants to use you?

Chapter Seven

An Old Enemy with a New Name
(Esther 3)

1. How was Haman "an old enemy with a new name"?

2. How is Haman an illustration of the Antichrist?

3. Do you agree that "what people do with authority is a test of character"? Give some examples.

4. When did Mordecai reveal that he was Jewish? Why?

5. How would the extermination of the Jews by Haman have changed history?

6. Do you agree with the practice of Christians getting involved in protest marches and rallies?

7. What do you think a Christian's practice should be regarding civil disobedience?

8. How did Haman use exaggeration to get his way?

9. Do you think apathy is a problem among Christians today? In what areas?

10. How do you see God's hand at work in this chapter of Esther?

Chapter Eight

A Day of Decision
(Esther 4)

1. "All that is required for evil to triumph is for good men to do nothing." How does that statement relate to Hitler's attempted extermination of the Jews?

2. What did Mordecai accomplish by mourning at the king's gate?

3. What was the important role Hathach played in the events taking place?

4. How would Esther have been negatively affected if she had done nothing to try to save her people?

5. Can you think of some other people that you believe God brought into prominence at special times to do special things?

6. "God accomplishes His purposes through people" (even ungodly ones). Do you agree? How does that make you feel about people and happenings in the world today?

7. Will our unwillingness to be used of God change His purposes? Explain.

8. Why is the fact that God is never in a hurry often hard for us to deal with?

9. How did Esther show her commitment to do God's will?

10. Esther "counted the cost" and chose to serve God. What kind of "cost" is involved in serving Him today?

Chapter Nine

A Day in the Life of the Prime Minister
(Esther 5)

1. What were the four forces that had begun to work together to destroy Haman?

2. "Preparing to pray is as important as the praying." What does that mean to you?

3. Do you think that crises are the usual way we are motivated to seek God? What else motivates you to pray?

4. Why didn't Esther immediately tell the king about Haman's evil plot?

5. What three evidences of God's sovereignty do you see at Esther's banquet?

6. "Pride is the ground in which all other sins grow, and the parent from which all the other sins come." Do you agree?

7. What is malice?

8. Why is a malicious spirit a dangerous thing to have?

9. Why is it important to balance prayer with action in the Christian life?

10. What changes do Christians need to be praying about and working toward in our world today?

Chapter Ten

Warning Signals
(Esther 6)

1. What evidences of God's sovereignty do you see in the king's sleepless night?

2. How has God directed you through seemingly minor incidents?

3. Through what book (other than the Bible) has God directed you at some time in your life?

4. What experiences in your life have shown you that God is in charge of schedules?

5. "God's delays are not God's denials," is sometimes hard for us to accept. What personal experience have you had of "delayed action" from God? How did you feel about it?

6. What is the irony of the king's reward to Mordecai?

7. How did the attention Mordecai received affect him?

8. How did Mordecai's reward affect Haman?

9. How did God warn Haman to stop what he was doing?

10. What do you think would have happened if Haman had heeded God's warning and repented?

Chapter Eleven

The Mask Comes Off
(Esther 7)

1. How is God's long-suffering and patience misinterpreted by the world?

2. What wrong assumptions did Haman make?

3. How did God help Esther with her petition to the king?

4. Do you think the king used Haman as a scapegoat? How?

5. How did Haman reap what he had sown? What are some other examples of that principle?

6. What is the positive side of reaping what we sow?

7. How does Haman's experience illustrate the futility of worldly riches?

8. What does Haman's experience teach us about the importance of godly character?

9. Why don't Christians need to wear masks to hide their pain or vulnerability?

10. "Every enemy that has ever tried to destroy Israel has been destroyed." What does that teach us about God's sovereignty?

Chapter Twelve

From Victims to Victors
(Esther 8)

1. Do you agree that "the only thing most of us know about sacrifice is how to spell the word"? Explain.

2. Why do you think the devil would like to get the church to stop praying?

3. How did what happened in Esther 8 correlate with God's promise to Abraham?

4. What could the church today learn from Mordecai and his couriers?

5. God will not change the law of Romans 6:23, but what other law has He made to save sinners?

6. What were the results of Mordecai's decree?

7. How did the feelings of Jews about themselves change through the events of the Book of Esther?

8. Do you think unbelievers are attracted to Jesus by your Christian joy?

9. If resources were not an obstacle, what would you like to do to help change the world for Christ?

10. Who would you like to have on your team to help you? Is there a specific group of people you would like to reach for Christ? Who are they?

Chapter Thirteen

God Keeps His Promises
(Esther 9-10)

1. Why had the Gentiles become afraid of the Jews?

2. "Instead of the godless world being afraid of the church, the church is afraid of the world." Do you agree? Explain.

3. Do you think that the church today is trying to use the weapons of the world to fight its battles? Give examples.

4. What weapons should the church be using?

5. "The church is always one generation short of extinction." What does that mean to you?

6. Explain the Feast of Purim which Jews celebrate.

7. What "celebrations" do Christians observe? Do you have personal or family celebrations for God's blessings?

8. Mordecai and Esther proved their commitment to God. What are some criteria we could use to evaluate our commitment to Christ?

9. How is the Book of Esther a good illustration of Romans 8:28?

10. How is Esther an example for all Christian women to follow?

Additional copies of this and
other Victor products are available
wherever good books are sold.

If you have enjoyed this book,
or if it has had an impact on your life,
we would like to hear from you.

Please contact us at:

VICTOR BOOKS
Cook Communications Ministries, Dept. 201
4050 Lee Vance View
Colorado Springs, CO 80918
Or visit our Web site:
www.cookministries.com

The Bible Teacher's Teacher